INTRODUCTION

You can have victory. You can arrive at a place in your life where you stop your unwanted sexual behaviors and begin to develop and maintain good ones. Whether you struggle with pornography, masturbation, sexually charged chat rooms, questionable mobile phone searches, or illicit, physical intercourse with others, you can find purity. You mature to a place where your heart and mind are clean. You can become the man or woman of integrity you long to be, where who you are on the outside matches who you are on the inside. You can be successful on your sexual purity journey. This book is the perfect place to start.

I have wrestled with sexual sin since my teenage years. On one hand, I lived a good, moral life. I sought to know God, find His will and follow Him. On the other hand, I struggled sexually. I looked at sensual magazines, searched for sexual content on the television (and then later on the computer), and masturbated. I had two lives - one on display for the world, and the other hidden and secretive. For a long time, I tried to be sexually pure, but never seemed to figure out how to get there.

In 2008, I started attending a sexual addiction support group and made regular appointments with a counselor who understood sexual struggles. The wise people I met with helped me understand several new truths about sexual purity. I think they'll be helpful to you too as you enter this *21-Day Purity Jumpstart.*

Sexual purity has to be learned. You don't come out of your childhood and adolescence knowing how to be sexually pure. It's a process. You have to be taught. Purity has to be modeled to you, and sometimes you will have to stumble, fall and get up a thousand times before you get there.

Consider this verse:

> *"It is God's will that you should be sanctified: that you should avoid sexual immorality; that each of you should <u>learn</u> to control your own body in a way that is holy and honorable, not in passionate lust like the pagans, who do not know God" I Thessalonians 4:3-5 NIV*

Sexual purity doesn't happen overnight. There is no magic solution to sexual purity. There are no "5 Easy Steps to Sexual Purity." There is not a singular insight, Bible verse, or prayer that will give you a shortcut to purity. It takes time.

Sexual purity requires the help of God. Purity happens from the inside out. It is ultimately a matter of the heart. Only God can fix your heart, change your desires and help you heal. Purity is also a spiritual battle. Your sinful nature and fleshly desires are too powerful for you to fight on your own. You need God's Spirit to give you the power to resist, avoid, and fight sexual temptation.

Sexual purity requires the help of others. You cannot figure out sexual purity on your own. You need the help of wise people to help you learn, point out your blind spots, and guide you in the right direction. Whether your help comes from teachers, counselors, or individuals who have experienced the same issues, your journey is meant to be one that is shared.

Sexual purity is only a portion of answering God's call to purity.

> *"But among you there must <u>not be even a hint of sexual immorality, or of any kind of impurity</u>, or of greed, because these are improper for God's holy people." Ephesians 5:3*

God requires you to be pure in more than one way. Overcoming sexual impurity is just one portion of what God expects from you. He wants your entire being to move toward holiness. He wants your mind, heart, emotion, relationship, body and spiritual life to be fully dedicated to Him.

James 1:27 says it well:

> *"Religion that God our Father accepts as pure and faultless is this: to look after orphans and widows in their distress and <u>to keep oneself from being polluted by the world</u>." James 1:27*

Another version of this verse reads "to keep oneself unstained by the world." No stain. No pollution. He wants you to be pure, holy, righteous and dedicated to Him.

Although this book focuses on sexual purity, keep in mind there are other areas in your life that God mandates you cleanse as well.

Sexual purity starts with your commitment. There is no purity without a heart-level commitment. It doesn't matter if you have started over hundred times and failed each time, you need to start over and try once more to become successful. You may have tried many different ways to obtain purity, but you've not tried everything. There are still methods you haven't explored. The principles of this book will help you discover what pieces you're missing and what sexual purity strategies you can explore next.

God is committed to your sexual purity. He is cheering for you and will help you. Why not pause right now and ask Him to help you on this journey?

> *"Dear God, help me to commit to this journey. Give me Your wisdom. Show me Your power. Change my heart and help me to want to do whatever it takes to be sexually pure. Amen."*

THE BEST WAY TO READ THIS BOOK

This is not a long book. I designed it to be concise and to the point. I would suggest reading this book at least twice. You should read it quickly the first time through in order to get a treetop view of the purity journey. Then read the book again, but slower this time so that you can absorb the lessons of each day. The book is filled with action steps. It will take some time to put the principles from this book into motion. I have provided you with plenty of open space in this book to write your own thoughts, questions and action points.

In addition to this book, I have recorded video and audio teachings for each day. While you're reading the book, let me come along side you and provide you with personal coaching and inspiration. Each teaching is about 10 minutes long. Go to www.puritycoaching.com to download the videos and audio.

You can also go through this book with a friend, accountability partner, small group, or support group. Do your Purity Jumpstart with others. If you would like multiple copies for your group, send me an email, and I will be glad to give you and your group a discount code.

Enough with the introduction, let's get started!

Jeff Fisher
jeff@puritycoaching.com
Raleigh, North Carolina

Table of Contents

DAY 1 - COME OUT OF ISOLATION

I was asked recently in an interview, "What's the best piece of advice you can give someone who struggles with their sexual purity?"

Wow, one singular piece of best advice? I have notebook after notebook filled with quotes, tips, notes from counseling sessions, books, podcasts and tidbits that I've overheard in support groups. How about 50, 100, or 1000 best pieces of advice?

My answer to his question was, "A sexual struggler has to come out of isolation and talk about his struggles to safe people. If a person stays in isolation he will never find the freedom and purity God has available."

Isolation is deadly when it comes to your sexual purity journey.

Freedom comes when we share our secrets and our struggles with safe people. You will never be sexually pure until you break the ice, do the hard thing, and tell someone about it. In sexual purity, there are no Han Solos or Lone Rangers. We need the help of others in order to become pure and stay pure.

> **Day 1 Action Step** – Find someone safe to share your struggles with, and do it.

DO I REALLY NEED TO TALK TO OTHERS ABOUT MY STRUGGLES?

Yes. You really do need to talk with someone about your struggles. I could share with you several moral, relational, psychological and emotional reasons why it's good to talk with others about your struggles. But let me appeal to your spiritual side. I assume you want to be sexually pure (at least in part) because you want to honor God. Think about these points in your reflections today:

1. **Sexual sin is much stronger than you.**
It's easy to underestimate the power of your sinful, fleshly nature. Sin had such a grip on humankind that it took the death of Jesus to break its bonds. You can control your behavior for a while on your own strength, but you will always come up short when it comes to defeating sin. You have to reach in God's direction for a solution to the sinfulness of your heart. As you read these verses I want you to feel the gravity of sin's pull:

"But each person is tempted when they are <u>dragged away</u> by their own evil desire and enticed. Then, after desire has conceived, it gives birth to sin; and sin, when it is full-grown, gives birth to <u>death</u>." James 1:14-15

Your own evil desires drag you away and catapult you along the death path.

"For sin, seizing the opportunity afforded by the commandment, deceived me, and through the commandment put me to death." Romans 7:11

This is the apostle, Paul, speaking. Paul (a.k.a. Super Christian) is seized and deceived by his own sin.

How will you break free from sin's grip when you are isolating?

2. **God's Word calls you to community (The "one another" verses).**
The Bible is full of "one another" passages. You need spiritual people in your life to help you find freedom. Look at where healing comes from:

Therefore confess your sins to each other and pray for each other so that you may be <u>healed</u>. The prayer of a righteous man is powerful and effective. James 5:16

Healing comes from confessing to one another. What about breaking the grip of habitual sin? And how do you find strength and restoration?

"Brothers, if someone is caught in a sin, you who are spiritual should restore him gently. But watch yourself, or you also may be tempted. ² Carry each other's burdens, and in this way you will fulfill the law of Christ." Galatians 6:1-2

Freedom, restoration and relief from sin's grip comes from submitting to one another and depending on one another.

How can you isolate and obey the "one another" passages in the Bible?

3. You are hard-wired for relationships.

"The LORD God said, "It is not good for the man to be alone. I will make a helper suitable for him." Genesis 2:18

God has built you (and all mankind) for one another. Genesis 2 is a part of the Adam and Eve narrative, but it applies to you also. God tells you that being isolated in life is "not good." Satisfaction comes from connecting with others. Discipleship, support, counsel, guidance, love, and grace come from connection. You're built for connection. This is your true hardwiring.

How can you function at full relational capacity if you are shutting yourself off from others?

4. Sexual purity is a discipleship process.

You are struggling in the area of sexual purity. God wants you to succeed. Purity requires you to be a learner for a while. However, during this time, God will line up a string of individuals to teach you. Your teachers may come from your own group of friends and family members. They may come from a support group or small group. They may even come through a ministry like PurityCoaching.com, where you sign up for accountability and coaching.

For now, you are the disciple. As you become healthy sexually, God will use you to help others.

"Praise be to the God and Father of our Lord Jesus Christ, the Father of compassion and the God of all comfort, who comforts us in all our troubles, so that we can comfort those in any trouble with the comfort we ourselves receive from God." II Corinthians 1:3-4

"And the things you have heard me say in the presence of many witnesses entrust to reliable people who will also be qualified to teach others." II Timothy 2:2

Be encouraged by these verses! God is calling you to purity. He is calling you out of isolation and into one of the biggest pools of help you can imagine. And as you mature, He is will lead you to others who will need your help.

- ➤ **Day 1 Action Step** – Find someone safe to share your struggles with, and do it. Come out of isolation.

- ➤ Who do you have in your life right now that you consider a safe person?

- ➤ Who is someone you can "test the waters" with and share a little bit of your struggles with?

- ➤ Who do you need to set up an appointment with (counselor, minister, small group leader)?

- ➤ Who can you email and reach out to that can help you?

DAY 2 – BUILD A GOOD DEFENSE

The quickest way to get results in your sexual purity journey is to build a good defense.

A good Defense creates a barrier between you and the people, places and things that challenge your purity. Today will help you have a basic understanding of defense. Days 3-5 will assist you in expanding and deepening your defense.

To understand defense: eliminate, block, and slow down.

Eliminate Access – A complete cutting off of your access to the source.
Examples: Cut your internet, change from a smart phone to a dumb phone, cut cable, break off a relationship, delete your social media account

Block Access – Obstacles that prevent you and the source from getting together. Roadblocks.
Examples: Internet filters, password protect your computer, carry no cash, block television channels, "unfollow" a person or groups on social media

Slow Down Access – Obstacles that slow you down from getting connected with the source. Some call them hurdles. My accountability partner, Tom, calls these "speed bumps".
Examples: Shut down your laptop at night, leave your tablet in another room, take a different route home, change seats at a restaurant

Think about a football team's defense. When the opponent has the ball, the job of the defense is to prevent the enemy from advancing, force negative yardage, and attempt to steal the ball. The defense puts forth maximum effort to keep the opposing team away so that the offense can do its job.

Your sexual purity defense should do the same things:

1. Prevent the source of struggle from getting to you
2. Give you breathing room to work your offense (talked about in Day 6)

You want to get points on the scoreboard when it comes to your sexual purity journey. You want to advance, you want to grow and you want to win. You will win by having a good offense, but first, you have to strengthen your defense.

PROBLEMS WITH DEFENSE ONLY

You will stumble on your purity journey if you focus on your defense only. Here's why:

You can't block out every bad influence - There are no perfect filters or blocks. Even if you throw your computer out of the window, you can always find a computer somewhere else. If you are determined to find a source to view sexual content you can find it.

Defense addresses the external, not the internal – Even if you were able to completely block out the people, places and things that tempted you sexually, you would still struggle in your heart. Sexual purity is a heart problem, not a behavior problem. Your defense will keep the temptations at a distance. Your offense will help you bring in all of those things that will aid you in becoming sexually pure.

Defense focuses on the "Do Not's" – Of course, you need to pay attention to the "do not's". The Ten Commandments are very relevant. The Bible is full of "do not" commands. But the Bible also has many "do" commands. Look for them the next time you're reading your Bible (see Ephesians 3 and Colossians 3). The "do's" are just as important as the "do not's".

The Pharisees in the New Testament were defense-only people. They loved the Law. They set up extra rules and regulations to keep them from breaking the Law, but they did not have a heart for the Law. They focused on the external and neglected the internal. Jesus had strong words for their defense-only focus.

> *"Woe to you, teachers of the law and Pharisees, you hypocrites! You clean the outside of the cup and dish, but inside they are full of greed and self-indulgence. Blind Pharisee! First clean the inside of the cup and dish, and then the outside also will be clean."* Matthew 23:25-26

A defense-only focus is out of balance. *The 21-Day Purity Jumpstart* will help you work through principles that will give you a balanced purity strategy. If you stick with it through these three weeks and work through the action points, you won't have to worry about being off centered in your purity focus.

You need to spend some time on today's action point. Don't blow through it. Take the time to build a good defense.

> ➢ **Day 2 Action Step** – Work on your defense today. Write down what you need to do to build up a good blockade.

> ➢ Q: What sources trip you up the most?

> ➢ Q: What steps do you need to take to:

Eliminate Access –

Block Access –

Slow Down Access –

DAY 3 - CLEAN HOUSE

What do you need to do in order to get rid of those things that are holding you back in your sexual purity journey?

Let's talk house cleaning today. Today is the day you need to look at the junk you're keeping around and make a commitment to throw it out for good.

> "...let us throw off everything that hinders and the sin that so easily entangles. And let us run with perseverance the race marked out for us, fixing our eyes on Jesus, the pioneer and perfecter of faith." Hebrews 12:1-2

CHECK THE NOUNS

A great purity tip to learn is: Check the nouns. You know what a noun is. It's a "person, place or thing." There are people, places, and things that influence you the wrong way. You need to eliminate or minimize your contact with them.

Checking the nouns is a form of defense. You need to get rid of the bad people, places and things.

Checking the nouns will also be an offensive purity tactic. Day 6 will guide you through building your offense. You need to invest in good people, places and things.

Get rid of the bad, and replace it with the good. People in addiction recovery circles might say, "You need to replace bad habits and behaviors with good habits and behaviors." This is very much a biblical principle.

> "Set your minds on things above, not on earthly things." Colossians 3:2

> "Therefore each of you must put off falsehood and speak truthfully to your neighbor, for we are all members of one body." Ephesians 4:25

➢ **Day 3 Action Step:** Take inventory of the people, places, things and media that are tripping you up. Circle or write out what nouns you need to get rid of.

PEOPLE

- People you have been sexual with
- Old girlfriends/old boyfriends
- Current girlfriend/current boyfriend
- Flirty people
- Chat rooms

- Email addresses
- Social media contacts
- Secret email accounts/Secret PO Box
- Secret bank account
- Other _____

PLACES

- Movie theater
- Porn shops
- Strip clubs
- Beach/Swimming Pools

- Casinos
- Concerts
- Restaurants/Bars/Hangouts
- Other _____

THINGS

- Magazines
- Catalogues
- Newspapers
- Mail outs/Flyers

- Clothing around the house
- Sex toys
- Alcohol
- Other _____

MEDIA

- Phone
- Tablet
- Work Computer
- Home Computer
- Radio/Satellite Radio
- TV/Cable/Satellite/DVR
- DVDS/Blu Rays/Rentals
- Netflix/Hulu/Amazon Prime
- Flash Drives
- Apps on your phone
- Podcasts
- Music
- Other _____

GET HONEST WITH YOURSELF

This is a self-assessment. You need to be as honest with yourself as possible. Admit that the bad nouns in your life are causing you to stumble. They are dragging you down. Be a man! Be a woman! Step up to the plate and call yourself out on the things that trip you up.

GET RADICAL, TURKEY!

You need to take radical measures to stop your bad behaviors. I'm guessing you've tried to stop some of your behaviors in the past. Maybe you've tried to end a relationship, or stop viewing certain sites on your phone. It hasn't worked very well, has it? We can't coexist with the bad nouns if we want to walk in God's direction.

You need to adopt the attitude of, "I'm willing to do whatever it takes to get better with sexual purity. I'm willing to let go of whatever is dragging me down in order to get there."

> *"You have heard that it was said, 'You shall not commit adultery.' But I tell you that anyone who looks at a woman lustfully has already committed adultery with her in his heart. If your right eye causes you to stumble, gouge it out and throw it away. It is better for you to lose one part of your body than for your whole body to be thrown into hell. And if your right hand causes you to stumble, cut it off and throw it away. It is better for you to lose one part of your body than for your whole body to go into hell." Matthew 5:27-30*

Jesus calls us to radical obedience when it comes to the things that trip us up. Cold turkey is the only way to go with bad nouns. Don't minimize or rationalize your friendship with them. Don't try to negotiate a limited relationship with them. Gouge it out! Cut it off! Throw it away! Those are radical statements.

MAKE A COMMITMENT

You need to make a fresh commitment to clean house. Identifying is great, but you need to follow through. It doesn't matter if you have made a commitment 1000 times before; you need to make another one.

We are three days in, and I'm already calling you to some big action plans. Are you with me? Let's keep this thing going! I'm going to continue to show you key purity principles that will help you keep your commitment and enhance it. If you want to be sexually pure for the long haul, you have to be ready to look and feel different. Pound out these action points and I'll see you on Day 4.

> **Day 3 Action Step:** Take inventory of the people, places, things and media that are tripping you up.

> **Day 3 Action Step:** Do it! Clean house.

DAY 4 - SET UP INTERNET PROTECTION AND RULES

You're not going to get far on your sexual purity journey until you have a strong Internet strategy.

Today, you need to focus on your home computer, your work computer, mobile phone, tablet, and any other device that you use to browse the Internet. You have to deal with your Internet interactions aggressively.

Your Internet strategy is part of your defense. It is full of roadblocks that must be set up, and may be part of your house cleaning from Day 3. Sometimes you have to get rid of the things that have control over you.

INTERNET DEFENSE

Let's look at several lines of defense for your Internet:

CONTENT FILTERS – This is the security software that prevents bad things from coming in. On practically all computers, you can go to the Internet Settings and adjust the level of security protection. However, you really need an extra level of security. There are many basic content filters available. Some people like programs such as, McAfee, Norton, AVG or Kaspersky. CNET.com is a good place to look at a list of options, some of which are free!

> **Day 4 Action Step:** Make sure your content filtering is up-to-date and you know how to use it.

ACCOUNTABILITY FILTERS – I am a big fan of accountability software. This is software that tracks all of the sites that you browse on the computer and reports them to one or more accountability partners. Accountability software is a wonderful innovation that has helped many men and women find an openness and freedom in using their devices.

➤ **Day 4 Action Step:** Try out one accountability filtering option.

Here are three great ones, and a commercial for my favorite:

> Covenant Eyes – www.covenanteyes.com
> X3Pure - www.x3pure.com
> K9 Web Protection - http://www1.k9webprotection.com/

I am really fond of Covenant Eyes. Our family uses their filtering and accountability software for all of our devices. They have been a good ministry partner with us. If you use our code, PURITY, at checkout, you can get your first month for free!

GIVE SOMEONE ELSE THE PASSWORD – If you know the password to your filtering and accountability software, you have a loophole. Let a friend set the password. If you're married, let your spouse be the only one who knows the password.

NO UNSUPERVISED INTERNET USE – This is a good step for those who cannot be trusted on the Internet. Make sure someone else is in the room when you are using your device. Another set of eyes will help you stay accountable. You may want to consider making a rule for yourself that will not allow you to get on the Internet unless someone else is there to supervise you.

GET RID OF THE INTERNET OR DEVICES WITH ACCESS – Extreme? You bet! If you have had major problems with the Internet and have proven yourself untrustworthy, this may be the only solution. You should not have to be off of the computer forever, but an abstinence period from the Internet could be the best thing to help you become healthier with your computer use.

BLACKLIST SITES – Some software gives you the ability to block specific sites that are bound to get you in trouble. If YouTube, Instagram, or a specific blog is a source of temptation, place it on a blacklist. Blacklisting requires a password for some devices. If your device does not require a password, blacklisting will take discipline on your part.

WHITELIST SITES – Good software has a whitelist option. This blocks all sites on a device except for the ones that you have deemed permissible for you to visit. While this is an especially great tool to use for young children who have access to the computer, it can also be extremely helpful for sexual strugglers.

INTERNET RULES

ONLY USE THE COMPUTER IN A PUBLIC PLACE – This is a good strategy for those who are either single or traveling. Go to the library. Go to an open table in a coffee shop or restaurant. Only use your computer where others can plainly see your screen.

STAY OFF THE COMPUTER AT VULNERABLE TIMES – This is a good rule for all who struggle. Alone times can be purity killers as well as certain times of the day. Make a commitment to your spouse or to a friend that you will not be on the computer during the following times:

- Early in the morning
- Late at night
- When you're alone
- After your spouse has gone to bed

DECEPTIVE WORKAROUNDS – There are many workarounds and cheats when it comes to an Internet defense. If you work in I.T. or are well-versed with computer technology, you know many of them. Some of you see blocks and defenses as challenges. The more blocks you put up, the more determined you will be to circumvent them. If you find yourself looking for ways to get around the defense you have put in place to aid you on your journey to spiritual purity, then it shows you just how much of a heart problem you really have.

Any effort made to cover your tracks or sneak sensual content into your daily routine should be considered deceptive. If you are working with an accountability partner, you need to cover this deception with a good accountability question. Here are a few Internet actions I consider deceptive:

- Wiping your history
- Deleting your cache
- Uninstalling and reinstalling blocking software
- Trying to figure out passwords
- Workarounds
- In-app browsing
- Installing/uninstalling apps that are triggers
- Image searching
- Social media searching
- Accessing computers or networks you know are not protected
- Searching on public computers
- Going through backdoors and/or trying to find backdoors

You will need to make your own list and come up with your own personal rules.

As I've said before, the battle is not going to be won on the defensive side. Defense helps you block and slow the bad content from seeping into your life. It also helps slow <u>you</u> down from seeking out the bad content.

Work on these action points today:

➢ **Day 4 Action Step:** Start building the layers of defenses around your Internet devices.

➢ **Day 4 Action Step:** Figure out what rules you need to have with your Internet devices.

And ask God to help you with your Internet defense:

"God, help me build a good strategy for my Internet and devices. Help me deep in my heart to want to be pure. Help me to be radical. Help me to be truthful with myself and with others about my Internet usage. Amen."

DAY 5 – GO TO THE PURITY GYM

Welcome the weightlifting portion of the Jumpstart program.

Some people who go the gym want to get big and strong. They want to bulk up and lift heavier weights. Others want to get lean and burn fat. They want to be thinner and faster. They want to be able to do more with less. You have been given a membership to the sexual purity gym. To succeed for the long haul, you're going to need to build strength, become efficient and develop endurance.

With strength – You will be able to say no to ungodliness and worldly passions. You will mature in your faith and purity. You will no longer act like a selfish child, but as a self-less, healthy adult instead.

With efficiency – You will be able to take the quicker path to healthy and godly passions. You will be able to do more with what you have. You will be able to maximize your creativity and energy so that you can bring God the most glory.

With endurance – You will be able to maintain sobriety longer. You will be able to withstand more challenges, pain and suffering and come out victorious. You will be able to see that God's goals for your life are more important than the momentary pleasures that sexual sins bring you.

CONTINUE TO SHOW UP

I think fifty percent of the purity battle is showing up.

We have a rule in our men's purity groups that is as follows: "Good, bad or ugly, we show up." You need to come to meetings regardless of what kind of week you've had. You're not going to get better if you don't show up consistently every week.

What do you need to show up to?

- Support group meetings
- Accountability meetings
- Meetings with your counselor, coach or wise person
- Church, Bible study or small group meetings
- Personal time with God
- Conversations with your spouse
- Hangout times with friends

You need to show up to the relational appointments that are going to propel your purity journey. You might look at this list and not have any of these appointments to show up to. That's okay. We will talk about all of them in this Jumpstart program. For now, the principle I want you to commit to is showing up. I want you to commit to showing up regardless of what struggles may come your way.

It's easy to show up when you're doing well. If you have had a week where your lines were not crossed and there were no major slip-ups, then showing up to an purity-meeting is not hard. It's much harder to show up when you've had a lot of struggles and are feeling ashamed.

There are a lot of times when you are not going to feel like showing up. There will be times when you have a bad day. Those are the days where you will receive the greatest benefit from showing up. If you can learn to show up when it's not easy, God will continue to strengthen you on your journey and honor your efforts.

➢ **Day 5 Action Step:** Make a commitment to yourself and to God that you will show up whether things are good, bad, or ugly.

PRACTICE SAYING NO TO UNGODLINESS

Saying no flies in the face of the sexual struggler. As a struggler, you have a long history of doing whatever you want to and pursuing whatever you desire. You have practiced saying yes to:

- Indulging in your fleshly desires
- Going to whatever sites you want to on the Internet
- Lusting after anyone you're attracted to and fantasizing about them
- Viewing whatever shows you want on TV and in the movies
- Doing whatever you want with your body

The spirit of God changes everything. He gives us a newfound ability to say no and calls us to a life of self-control. Here is Paul talking to Titus:

> "For the grace of God has appeared that offers salvation to all people. It teaches us to say "No" to ungodliness and worldly passions, and to live self-controlled, upright and godly lives in this present age," Titus 2:11-12

Peter says it as well:

> "I urge you, as foreigners and exiles, to abstain from sinful desires, which wage war against your soul." I Peter 2:11

Jesus tells us to say No in the form of denial:

> "Whoever wants to be my disciple must deny themselves and take up their cross and follow me." Mark 8:34

Saying no begins with a relationship with Jesus. - You do not have the power within yourself to say no to sexual sin for the long-term. Eventually, your strength will run out and you will fail. Only Jesus can give you the ability to say no. You need to make sure you are connected to Him. Make sure you're connected to the power source that can help you say no.

> ➤ **Day 5 Action Step:** Make sure you have a relationship with Jesus.

I have put a special chapter in the back of this book about salvation. This chapter is designed to help you with the basics of what it means to have a relationship with Jesus.

Small "No's" lead to bigger "No's." - As you practice saying no, you will get better at it. You start with what's in front of you. Build your defense. Set up roadblocks. Set up good rules and boundaries. Say no to the bad things that are in front of you right now. They will prepare you for the bigger battles down the road. The guy new to the gym starts with the 10 lb. weights before he can move up to the 50 lb. weights.

You must say no 1000 times. – Long-term purity builds up over time as you practice saying no. You need to practice consistently. Every time you say no to ungodliness you take another small step forward on God's path toward sexual purity. Say no and repeat. Wash, rinse and repeat, right?

Saying no means sacrifice. - It hurts to deny myself. It hurts to say no, especially if I am used to getting what I want. There is always sacrifice with self-discipline. I choose to say no now, so I can say yes to something greater.

I'm sure you didn't pick up this book expecting me to tell you to suffer. You wanted a 21-day solution to your sexual struggles and you wanted it to be easy. I wish it were easy. I wish there was a pathway to sexual purity that didn't involve pain, challenge and suffering.

You won't be able to get stronger, become more efficient or build endurance without suffering. Think about the body builder. He shows up for his workouts religiously. He works his muscle groups by challenging them and pushing them to the point of fatigue. Then he rests, rehydrates, downs a whey powder banana shake and goes after it again. He does the hard work, but he's got a bigger goal in mind.

Saying no to short-term pleasure gives you the opportunity to say yes to long-term fulfillment.

Let's talk about God's greater plan.

PRACTICE SAYING YES TO GOD'S GREATER PLAN

Saying no and denying self gets easier when you have a larger goal in mind. The bodybuilder thinks about his future physique. A runner thinks about finishing his race with a great time. The dieter thinks about fitting into a smaller pant or dress size.

<u>Sexual purity brings a payoff for you</u>. You will be healthy, whole, and not controlled by your urges. Purity will affect you emotionally, mentally, physically, and most importantly, spiritually.

<u>Sexual purity brings a payoff in your relationships.</u> You will be able to give more of yourself to your family, friends and others. You will be able to understand what true intimacy in your relationships look like. You will learn to respect and value others.

<u>Sexual purity brings a payoff for the Kingdom of God.</u> You will not have a divided heart. You will be able to serve God with integrity. Your sexuality, emotions, relationships and thought life will honor Him.

If you can get a glimpse of His greatness, His grace, His love and His plan for you, it will help you say no. The more you know God, the more you'll come to understand that the rewards are much bigger when you decide to live by His rules. God doesn't ask you to deny yourself and your fleshly desires to punish you. He has a better path in mind for you. God knows that the path of our evil desires will lead to death and destruction. He wants to preserve us from that. God wants to save you from regrets and foolish decisions.

> *" See, I set before you today life and prosperity, death and destruction. For I command you today to love the LORD your God, to walk in obedience to him, and to keep his commands, decrees and laws; then you will live and increase, and the LORD your God will bless you in the land you are entering to possess." Deuteronomy 30:15-16*

➤ **Day 5 Action Step:** Why are you saying yes to God? What's the bigger picture you're shooting for? What are your motivations? Write your reasons below.

DAY 6 – BUILD A GOOD OFFENSE

A good sexual purity strategy requires a strong defense and a strong offense. The battle for sexual purity is won on the offensive side. Today you will learn the difference between a purity defense and a purity offense and get some practical action points on building your offense.

Defense keeps the bad stuff out (or at least slows it down). It keeps you from being overrun by triggers, temptations and attacks of the Enemy. Defense eliminates obstacles to purity, positions roadblocks, and sets up hurdles. Defense manages the external so that you can focus on the internal.

Offense brings in the good stuff. It pursues healthy people, places and things. It makes forward progress. Offense is actively seeking to heal, grow, build, strengthen, and stretch. Do whatever you can to "beef up" your offense.

Building your offense might seem like a daunting task to you at first. Offense focuses heavily on good relationships. Those can be hard if you don't have many friends and have chosen to isolate yourself from others. Offense seeks out healthy alternatives. This is a new effort for a person who doesn't have any hobbies or creative projects. You will have to work harder on the front end to try new things. It will take a while to get used to reaching out in healthy directions. Identify two or three new steps you can take to build your offense, and start working on them.

Here are seven areas you can work on that will help you build your offense. I have given you a few examples under each one to get you thinking. Take some time under each action point to write out ways you can build your offense.

SEVEN OFFENSE BUILDERS

1. **Relationships – Start and Strengthen Them** – Build your existing relationships with your friends, your support team and your spouse. Do more with the people you know who are helpful, encouraging, supportive, and loving. If you don't have many friends, you need to take some intentional steps to make new friends. Consider reaching out to church members, small group members, schoolmates, and even family members and neighbors.

Action Step: Pick one or two of your existing friends, and start hanging out with them more.

Action Step: Break the ice on making a new friend this week. Consider joining a club, small group Bible study, special interest group or gym to meet new people.

2. **Healing – Find People to Help You** – Our hearts need God's healing. We all have been hurt so badly in our past that it led to damage. Our wounds might be deep anger, disappointment, resentment, negative messages, grief or abuse. Deeper healing helps us grow stronger on the inside. You might find facing the pain with a counselor, minister or someone who has found healing from sexual struggles to be therapeutic.

Action Step: Make an appointment with a counselor or minister to talk about your deeper issues.

3. **Spiritual Life – Feed it** – Work on your relationship with God. You need His power to help you. Schedule Bible reading and prayer time with Him. Go places that encourage you to learn more about God. This is where church, small groups, men and women's ministries and Bible-based conferences can help you in your spiritual growth.

Action Step: Start a Bible reading and prayer time.

Action Step: Make a commitment to yourself to visit a church or small group this week.

4. **Serve, Volunteer and Mentor – Look for Opportunities** – One of the best ways to get your focus off of yourself is to start helping others. You're not a purity expert yet, but you can share your story. Your story is powerful and so is your life. Share your life with others. Volunteer through your church or a non-profit organization. When you are giving of yourself and loving, it is impossible to be selfish and consuming. Reversing the flow from selfish to serving will have a huge effect on your sexual health.

Action Step: Research an opportunity to volunteer or serve others. Look for something in the next month or two and sign up.

5. **Mind and Heart – Challenge It** – Take your mind and heart to places they've never been before. Look for a book that will stretch you. Start writing in a journal or on a blog that will stretch your mind. Your heart is challenged as you open it to new people and new experiences. It might mean going on a trip with your kids and doing something special for them. Maybe participating in a marriage conference is something additional that you and your spouse could consider signing up for.

Action Step: Purchase a new book that will stretch your mind and challenge you. Schedule a trip or adventure that takes you to a new place.

6. **Faith – Challenge It** – What are you doing that requires you to walk by faith? It must be something that is impossible for you in your efforts and resources. What is impossible for us is possible with God. Your faith decision might be a giving decision that stretches you. It might be signing up for a mission trip. It might be sponsoring a child. It might be starting a new job. When we go through life by faith, we are forced to rely on God. Your faith will be challenged many times as you seek to be sexually pure. You have to learn to lean on Him for the strength. What I'm asking you to do is intentionally choose something that will challenge you to depend solely on Him.

Action Step: Look for an opportunity that will stretch your faith, and commit to it.

7. **Creativity and Passion – Express It.** - You are a passionate, creative person. God made you that way. You have spent a lot of your time, energy, passion, creativity and money on lustful habits. You need to find healthy places for that energy. Take up a hobby. Build something. Create and innovate. Learning to steer yourself in healthy directions when you feel like giving into sinful desires is a huge step. You have to learn to think differently with your creativity.

Action Step: Start or restart one project or hobby. Make sure it's fun and something you can pour yourself into with passion.

Can you see how building your offense will help you? When you feel tempted and triggered to sin sexually, you will have a lot of healthy alternatives to pour yourself into. You will learn to find greater fulfillment in relationships, creativity, and work projects than you would with pornography. You will also learn that when your spirit, heart and mind are stretched with new challenges, God will fill you with His strength. Your resistance to sexual sin will grow. Internally you will get stronger. And you will find it easier to be pure and stay pure.

DON'T BE OFFENSE ONLY

Be careful not to focus so much on offense that you neglect your defense. You can get so wrapped up in yourself, your heart condition, and your relationships that you forget to set up the necessary roadblocks.

Any of the seven offensive action steps above can be blown out of proportion. You need relationships, but don't make them your sole purity solution. It's the same with counseling. Reflective work and healing from the wounds of the past is important, but make sure you are utilizing several of the offensive strategies I suggested.

BEWARE OF THE HYPER-SPIRITUAL SOLUTION TO PURITY

The people that get out of balance with their purity the quickest seem to be the hyper-spiritual people.

There are some who believe sexual purity can be achieved through more religious action. They say if you read your Bible more, fast, pray, go to confessional, go to mass or memorize enough verses, you will find the cure. These are the same people who believe reading the works of Jonathan Edwards, Charles Spurgeon and C.S. Lewis provide some magical key to being a super-Christian.

I agree that God needs to be larger in your life and that you must rid yourself of spiritual idols. But you can't be spiritual enough on your own to overcome sexual sin. The super-spiritual seem to think it all depends on them.

Above, in Action steps 3 and 6, I challenged you to feed your spiritual life and stretch your faith. When you are deeply connected to God and other spiritual people, it will propel your spiritual life and help you become pure. Be God-centered in everything you do. Let Christ and His Word be at the center of your sexual purity journey. Allow God to use many skilled people and many creative pursuits to help you stay on His path of purity.

Go back to the action steps for today. Fill out as much as you can and begin putting them into practice.

DAY 7 – BUILD YOUR SUPPORT TEAM

I want you to take a moment today and assess your support team. Who's walking with you on your sexual purity journey? Who's providing support for you? Who's coming alongside you so that you don't feel like you're alone in the battle?

Your support team needs to be filled with three types of people:

1. General support
2. Specialty support
3. Drill-Down support

GENERAL SUPPORT

Most of your support team will be made up of general support. They will be people who know at least a little bit of your story and support you. They could be your spouse, friends, family, neighbors, church members, a minister or anyone who can show love to you and support your purity journey.

Support people need to be safe to talk to. It's okay for a person on your support team to challenge you, correct you or disagree with you, but they should not beat you up and tear you down with their words. Good support is built on trust. Good supportive people are reciprocal - you share, they share, and you both build up each other together.

Invite people to support you. Most of the time you are the one who will have to take the initiative. Be courageous. Step up to the plate and reach out. Start by sharing a little bit of your story. Test the waters and see if they are good for it.

Every best friend, accountability partner, soul mate, spouse and mud-walking friend starts out as general support. Most of your general support will be just that - <u>general</u> support. But God will cause some of your relationships to blossom into deeper support.

As you build your General Support team, look for people who:

1. Love you as you are – You need people who accept you – good, bad or ugly. These people are pro-you. They are happy when you are around. They will be people who fulfill the Bible's command to "love one another."

2. Talk about normal life things too – Do all aspects of life together, not just the hardships. Sometimes you need people to help you process hardships. Sometimes you need people who talk to you about normal life. Sometimes the need of the moment is to have fun together. Find people who are multi-dimensional in the way they relate to you. Two of my friends are in prison because of their sexual struggles. When I visit and write, we talk about their situations and their struggles if those are the needs of the moment. Most of our time is spent talking about normal life issues. We talk family, discuss sports and current events, share spiritual insights, and joke with one another.

3. Hang out together with – Add four or five guys you can build into your support team to watch the game with or go to the movies with. Ladies, find four or five gals you can have brunch with or share Pinterest ideas with.

4. Have common interests – You need to cultivate a few hobbies and share them with your buddies. It will be a very important part of your offensive strategy. Instead of going to bad places to do bad things with the wrong people, I go to good places to do better things with supportive people.

5. Go a little deeper – These people do know your story, or at least some of it. They need to be deep enough and know enough so that they can talk with you, support you, and pray for you. People who just talk about the weather or the sports game are not part of your support team.

➢ **Day 7 Action Step:** Make a list of people whom you would consider General Support.

➢ Where are the gaps in your General Support? Are your friends multi-dimensional enough?

SPECIALTY SUPPORT

These are people who help you with specific areas of purity and recovery - counselors, coaches, ministers, doctors and lawyers. They know your story and have special training and experience to assist you with specific areas. Specialty support is focused and fine-tuned to your individual needs.

Think about the aspects of your life: physical, emotional, spiritual, mental and relational. Your sexual struggles have affected each of these areas. There will be some (and maybe many) areas where you need specialty support.

Think of your specialty support people as private lesson teachers. I play trumpet and have taken lessons on many occasions. Early in my playing, I needed basic lessons. General lessons that may have applied to anyone. It didn't take long for my private lessons to turn into specialty coaching sessions. My teacher would help me with issues I was having with a music piece by building my range or improving my tone.

Physical – Sexual sin rewires our brain chemistry to seek sexual sin. I might need psychiatric help for this. If I have any type of disease or become an alcoholic or drug addict, I will need get some professional help from people who understand how to help resolve the issues of the body. Specialty support in this instance would include physicians, nutritionists, and exercise trainers.

Emotional – The hurts of the past may be keeping me down. I need healing. Or I have a very difficult patch of pain I can't work through. Your specialty support would be counselors, experienced leaders in the church, wise friends with experience, or maybe even counseling intensives.

Spiritual – Many have "God questions" about their sexual sin. "Why would God allow this to happen?", "Why did God make me this way?", "How could God love me after the things I've done?" *Ministers, Pastoral counselors, or wise spiritual people in your church would support you by* *providing answers to a lot of those questions you often find yourself thinking about.*   .

Mental – This is the intellectual side of our purity journey. We need to get education and wisdom from people who share similar stories. I need to find out what sexual addiction is and how it works. I need to expose my misunderstandings and correct the lies I believe about my struggles. Consulting book resources, viewing podcasts on purity, attending conferences, participating in workshops, purchasing helpful videos, and of course, browsing Puritycoaching.com are all support mechanisms that can be used for this aspect of your journey.

Relational – My relationships are all shot up. It turns out I was a different person on the inside. Now those who are closest to me are hurting. Trust is broken. I need specialty people who can help me repair relationships. For some, they may have never had many good relationships. The coaching they need is in how to make friends and cultivate healthy relationships. They can receive the help they need from *counselors, teachers, mediators and PurityCoaching.com.*

Legal – This is another person on our specialty support team we may not think about. If we have done something illegal or have serious questions about actions committed in our past, we need to seek legal advice. If we are facing a separation or divorce, we need legal counsel. If we have been a victim of a sexual crime, we will need to talk to the police and probably consult a lawyer.

> ➢ **Day 7 Action Step:** What about your Specialty Support team? Who's helping you in these areas?

Physical –

Emotional -

Spiritual –

Mental –

Relational –

Legal -

You don't need to fill out every blank. Only fill out the ones that you know you need to work on. Make sure that you think about what areas are broken and need fine-tuning.

> ➢ Q: Where are your gaps? What's the next area you need to focus on to find specialty support?

DRILL-DOWN SUPPORT

Your Drill-Down friends will be your deepest level of support. These people know most or all of your story. They accept you, support you and walk with you in your purity journey through thick and thin. They are your accountability partners. They are your friends. These are the people who are allowed to ask the hard questions and expect you to give an honest answer.

Day 12 of this book will help you more with accountability.

Let me give you a few tips on finding and developing your Drill-Down Support.

1. **Build your General Support and work your way upward** – Your Drill-Down support will come from your current friends and your future friends. You will find that the people who you have the best chemistry with will be those who are supportive of you and will be willing to invest in your life. These are potential Drill-Down candidates.

2. **Invite them to a Drill-Down Relationship** – Ask your friends to help you. Ask them if they would walk with you on a deeper level and touch base with you more frequently. Ask them if they would commit to meeting you each week to talk over a cup of coffee, a game of golf, or the featured ball game of the week. They can be a great asset to you.

3. **Share More of Your Story** – Test the waters. Offer a little more of your story and see how it goes. Open up with your friend about your vulnerable points. That's how trust is built.

Be patient as you are looking for Drill-Down Support. Give it some time. Ask God for His help. He wants you to find people with whom you can be transparent with, people you can run deeply with. Jesus invited Peter, James and John to share in the deeper levels of His life. Moses had Aaron and Joshua. Elijah had Elisha. Abraham had his son Isaac. Paul had Silas initially, and then added Timothy.

➢ **Day 7 Action Step:** Who's on your Drill-Down team? Or who has the potential to be Drill-Down for you?

➢ If you don't have a Drill-Down person, that's okay. Pause right now and ask God to bring someone like this in your life.

Resource Recommendation

If you're ready to work on building and enhancing your Drill-Down Support, the next resource you might want to look at is my *21-Day Accountability Jumpstart (out December 2015)*. This book will help you understand accountability, learn how to find accountability partners, and how to be accountable for the long haul.

DAY 8 – PRACTICE TRUTHFULNESS

Purity and truth are tied together. You can only be as pure as you are truthful. As a sexual struggler, you probably have a good amount of experience lying, covering up, hiding, telling half-truths, and deflecting the attention of others so you don't get caught. Today's purity focus is on truthfulness. Truth-telling is a simple principle, but it can be very challenging if you have a long history of not telling the truth.

Sit and absorb this scripture. Read it several times, slowly.

> *"Therefore each of you must put off falsehood and speak truthfully to your neighbor, for we are all members of one body." Ephesians 4:25*

Quit lying. Practice telling the truth. You honor God when you tell the truth, and you also show love and respect for others.

FIVE REASONS YOU KEEP LYING

1. **You Think It's Better to Lie** – You believe that there are times when you will do more damage to yourself and others if you tell the truth. "Why should I hurt my spouse by telling her about my actions? It would just make things worse, or destroy our marriage."

Reality: Lies only feed the darkness. Lies are sin and take you away from God. Lies break trust in your relationships. You may hurt others by telling the truth, but you will never be able to be authentic and have integrity with others if you consistently lie.

You Try to Keep People Out of Your Business – You might not want anyone to get close to the truth of your life. You tell them "my business is my business." In the name of privacy, you deflect the attention of others. This is a type of untruthfulness.

Reality: Your problems do affect others. And the closer they are to you, the more your lying affects them. Your ability to have healthy relationships and a healthy sexuality depends on your truthful connections with others. It's called intimacy.

2. **You Want Others to Believe You're OK** – Your pride can keep you from being truthful as well as the shame you feel about yourself over your secret behaviors. You maintain a good outward appearance to protect the inner you that no one sees.

Reality: Others have problems just like you do. No one is perfect or free from hurt. God's healing comes when you are in close contact with others. Admitting you have weaknesses is a sign of strength. You should never look at it as a character flaw.

3. **You Believe if You Tell the Truth You Will Be Punished** - There were probably times in your past when you told the truth and got in trouble for it. You lied to protect yourself and it seemed to be the best solution to your problem at that time.

Reality: God values truthfulness, and ultimately, your friends do too. No one wants to be lied to or deceived. Your workplace values truth. Your spouse and kids value truth. Relationships are built on trust and truthfulness. Yes, punishment and consequences may come from telling the truth, but the consequences will be much greater if you continue to deceive others and are found to be untruthful.

4. **You Believe Your Problem Will Eventually Go Away** –You believe that if you cover up your problem by lying to others, your issues will slowly fade away with time.

Reality: Your sexual problems are often worse than you think they are. They won't go away. They grow in your heart and fester. Lying compounds and complicates your problems. You have to continue lying to keep your secrets and often come up with more creative lies to maintain your cover. You will not be free from your bondage to lying until you start telling the truth.

> **Day 8 Action Step:** What are ways you have lied about your struggles?

> **Day 8 Action Step:** What fears do you have about telling the truth about your struggles?

> Take a moment to be honest with God about your fears in prayer. Talk to God about them.

THE TRUTH WILL COME OUT

At first, your secrets are easily contained, but as your struggles grow they affect other parts of your life (work, relationships, performance, etc.) and are harder to maintain. You get deeper in your lying and have more to cover up. You will be able to keep up the façade for a while, but eventually…

- You will slip.
- You will be caught in your lies.

- You will become careless or callous.
- You will be exposed by God.

"A false witness will not go unpunished, and he who pours out lies will perish." Proverbs 19:9

HOW DO YOU FIX IT?

Lying can only be fixed when we value truthfulness and practice it.

<u>Value Truthfulness</u> - You have to <u>want</u> to tell the truth. You have to believe that the temporary discomfort of telling the truth is better than the long-term consequences of continuing to lie.

➢ **Day 8 Action Step:** Valuing truthfulness is a matter of the heart. If you're not there, God is the only one who can help you get there. Talk to Him about it. Spend time with Him in prayer and ask Him to change your heart.

<u>Practice Truthfulness</u> – This takes courage. God can help with this too.

Start by telling the truth with people who are safe or sworn to confidentiality: A counselor, a minister, or someone who can keep your trust. Reach out to me by email at jeff@puritycoaching.com. I would be glad to be a person you practice your truthfulness with.

➢ **Day 8 Action Step:** Who have you lied to about your struggles?

➢ Who do you need to make amends with?

➢ Who is somebody safe you know that you can practice telling the truth with?

Bonus Content: On the video and audio resources, I give you some advanced tips on truthfulness when I talk about the Principle of Flush and Flow. I also talk about the time my friend, Tim, taught me the value of "bringing things out into the light."

You can find the link to these videos at our website: www.puritycoaching.com.

DAY 9 – NAVIGATING SLIPS AND RELAPSES

Two terms you hear a lot about in the world of sexual purity and sexual addiction are *slip* and *relapse*. There is a difference between a *slip* and a *relapse*.

Slip – When you cross a sexual purity line you don't want to cross.

Relapse – When you keep crossing your purity lines and stay there.

LET'S TALK ABOUT SLIPS

A slip may be a one-time event or a binge that lasts for several hours. You cross your purity line, but you bounce back quickly and <u>return</u> to recovery. Slips are part of the purity process. No one goes from a point of "awakening" to complete sobriety. Purity happens gradually, and comes with many ups and downs.

You are responsible for your slips, of course. There are consequences that come with every slip, sometimes big and sometimes small. If you learn to take your sin seriously (talked about more in Day 16), you will see slips as a big deal.

Slips happen while a person is in recovery, but they do no throw him out of recovery. If you are taking three steps forward, slips are considered the two steps back. My friend and accountability partner, Tom, says it this way, "Your recovery train may take a detour with slips, but it still keeps going. A relapse, on the other hand, is when your train goes completely off the track and stays there."

Slips may be normal for the purity process, but they are still slips. They are still steps in the wrong direction. You are still responsible. They are still sins that must be dealt with. Remember, all sin comes with a range of consequences that must be faced.

YOU HAD A SLIP. WHAT'S NEXT?

1. **Stop acting out** – This is common sense. Stop your bad behaviors. Take the first step in the right direction.

2. **Confess it to someone** – Bring your behavior out into the light. Whether it's a small slip or a larger one, you need to talk about it. This is a huge strategy for building up strength for next time.

3. **Repent** – Repentance means that you make a U-Turn in your behavior and in your attitude. Commit to walk the other way and follow through.

4. **Build hedges and support around your trigger areas** – Set up roadblocks and accountability around the areas of your struggle. Craft out a creative, fresh strategy to combat your vulnerabilities.

IS THIS A ONE-TIME ISSUE OR A REPEAT OFFENDER?

Some triggers, temptations and slips will be new to you. A new person may come across your path that catches your attention. Or you may watch a TV show and be surprised by a sex scene. Bring new struggles into the light, and adjust your purity strategy. But if you are coming back to this same slip (repeat offender), more drastic measures have to be put in place.

➢ **Day 9 Action Step:** What are you doing to make sure your slips don't turn into repeat offenders?

➢ What's your strategy for handling slips?

LET'S TALK ABOUT RELAPSE

When you relapse, you return to your old, impure lifestyle and stop being active on your purity journey. You may still meet with your accountability partners, group, or counselor, but you are just going through the motions. You stop being honest about your behaviors, you minimize your sin, and you don't do much to prevent your bad sexual behaviors. In essence, you have stopped fighting and have given up.

THE RELAPSE GETS WORSE

A relapse begins as a slip, but progresses quickly into a full-blown lifestyle. A cascade of slips will draw you back into your former bondage. Slips increase from occasional to frequent.

In relapse, you start hiding things again. You will restart old patterns. You might start contacting people you've had sexual relationships with before.

In relapse, you start faking it. When you slip, you put on a false front so others don't find out and don't ask. You might be able to fool your group or counselor for a while, but eventually you're going to stop caring. Eventually, someone's going to be smart enough to ask the right questions and your cover will be blown.

In relapse, you disconnect from the 4 S's. You stop connecting with your support team. You stop working your offense and defense. You loosen your structure and miss meetings. And you go dry in your spiritual life, failing to connect with God and others who love God.

In relapse, you feel a sense of hopelessness and start believing lies. You may think:

"Well, now I've really messed up! I might as well give up."
"It's no use. I'll never get free of this."
"I'm better off in this lifestyle anyway."

"I'll save people a lot of pain if I just stop talking to them."
"I guess I'm a lost cause."

I'M IN RELAPSE. WHAT NEXT?

1. **You have to want to be well** – If you've grown progressively worse in your struggles, something has to change. You have to get sick of your behaviors and sick of your condition again. Brokenness and a desire to be well have to come from deep inside, that's God's territory. This is where it's good to pray, "God help me to hate my sin again. Help me to <u>want</u> to get well."

2. **What triggered your relapse in the first place?** – It's important to do a little dissection and analysis here. Do this with the help of a counselor or mature friend. Trace the path that you took and the large and small slips that led to your relapse.

3. **You need others to huddle around you** – More than ever, you need support. You may have to call out for it or beg for it, but you need others to help you get strong again. A relapse means you have been crippled and weakened. You need others hovering around you to nurse you back to health and help you work through it.

4. **You need major accountability** – Finding people to hold you accountable is critical. No one can make you well. You can't force someone to <u>not</u> act out. If you want to act out, you're going to find a way to do it. But you need people to come alongside you as you walk in the light and help you stay focused. You need people who will speak truth into your life and help you work on the areas that you are failing in.

5. **You need the power of God** – Somewhere early in your slips you started ignoring God. You stopped surrendering and listening.

You've got to get back on track with your walk with God. You need to start talking to Him again, asking Him to bring you out of bondage, and letting go so that His power can come to your rescue. Sexual impurity is driven by core issues that God fully knows and has the power to change.

- **Day 9 Action Step:** What action steps do you need to take to get out of relapse?

- What is your relapse prevention strategy? Write out 5 or 6 preventative measures in the space below.

DAY 10 – GET WISE GUYS IN YOUR LIFE

Sexual purity is a learning process. You will not automatically become sexually pure over time. It requires discipleship, which means you need teachers and mentors to help you progress. You need to find wise people from whom can you glean experience from.

Consider yourself:
- A student in need of teachers.
- A rookie in need of veterans.
- An inexperienced person in need of experienced individuals.
- An immature struggler in need of mature people with a track record.

"Walk with the wise and become wise, for a companion of fools suffers harm." Proverbs 13:20

➤ **Day 10 Action Step:** Write down people you know or have heard about who might make good teachers for you.

➤ Wise friends who understand sexual struggles –

➤ Professional counselors –

➤ Purity ministries –

➤ Ministry leaders -

➤ Bible study leaders or small group leaders –

➤ Other -

Ask For Referrals – Start with the people you know. Ask friends to give you some names of people who would be good to talk with. Ask ministers where the counselors are. Ask counselors where to find support groups. Ask your Bible study teacher to recommend wise members in your church. Email purity ministries to see if they know good resources in your area.

Join a Support Group – A support group will give you an instant group of friends who understand your world. The group leader should know a few things about purity. Take him out to lunch. Buy him a cup of coffee. It's worth your time. Guys in support groups know who the good counselors are, what ministries are helpful, and where the safer churches are.

Be Persistent - You may have to dig and search for a while until you find the right people. Your first counselor may not work out. The wise person in your church you have a connection with may not have the time in his schedule to work with you. You may not get a response from a ministry leader for a while. Be intentional! Keep looking for the right people.

Spend the money – Appointments with professionals can be expensive. The right counselor or coaching or training conference can pay big dividends into your purity journey. Do what you can to get in front of the best people you can find. Even if the person you are meeting with is not a professional (who charges fees), buy his lunch or pickup his cup of coffee. Invest in your purity, and show appreciation for your wise guys.

Economic Tips
- Many counselors take insurance. Ask.
- If you commit to and pay in advance for several sessions, some counselors will give   you a discount.
- Scholarships are available for some training conferences and weekend intensives.
- Email the leader to see if he can bend on the price (he probably can).

- Use one of our puritycoaching.com discount codes. They are located in the back of this book.

Supplement with Books and Podcasts - A lot of mentoring can come from books and podcasts. Take advantage of the opportunities to learn from experienced writers. Go to ITunes or one of the podcast feeds to find podcasts on sexual purity. There are some really good ones out there. Sample a few. These resources are not as good as interacting with a live person, so keep looking for the right people, and supplement with written, audio and video resources.

Think Long-Term – The best training comes when you spend a lot of time with your teachers. Jesus walked with his disciples every day for three and a half years. Moses walked with Aaron and Joshua for over forty years. Paul took Timothy on several of his missionary journeys.

Train Others (When It's Time) – God will put others in your life who need help. You can share your story and what you're learning with anybody. You can listen to anybody. Taking on a disciple comes later as you mature in your purity journey.

> *"You then, my son, be strong in the grace that is in Christ Jesus. And the things you have heard me say in the presence of many witnesses entrust to reliable people who will also be qualified to teach others."* II Timothy 2:1-2

> *"Praise be to the God and Father of our Lord Jesus Christ, the Father of compassion and the God of all comfort, who comforts us in all our troubles, so that we can comfort those in any trouble with the comfort we ourselves receive from God."* II Corinthians 1:3-4

➢ **Day 10 Action Step:** Write your own action steps today. You know you need wise guys. You know whether or not you got 'em.

➢ What's next for you?

DAY 11 – BUILD YOUR STRUCTURE

Let's talk structure today.

Structure is any framework you set up to support your purity journey. Some examples are:

- Support group meetings
- Regular counseling appointments
- Boundaries for your computer use
- Hedges you build around relationships at work
- Personal rules about dating
- Travel boundaries
- Weekly accountability meetings
- Personal rules for alone time or bored time

Structure provides stability and protection. Structure promotes healing. Structure keeps you from being pulled off in wrong directions.

THINK – BROKEN BONE

If you broke your arm, you would go to the emergency room. The doctors would set your bone and put a cast around it. The cast will keep your arm in place so it can heal. The worse the break, the more measures need to be taken to give structure to the break. Think about your sexual purity structure in the same way. You have an area in your life that is broken. It needs skilled help, good structure and time to get healthy.

As a sexual struggler, you probably had very little structure. You didn't attend meetings with people who could disciple you in your purity. You were loose with your boundaries. You had little or no accountability. And you were hit or miss in your self-discipline. Most sexual strugglers have poor structure. Now you have an opportunity to learn the importance of structure and apply it to your life.

THREE EASY TYPES OF STRUCTURE & ONE TOUGH ONE

The easiest types of structure to set up will be:

1. Meetings – You need to meet with people on your support team. Your meetings might be support group meetings, counseling appointments, personal Bible study, group Bible study, men or women's group meetings, church worship, or hangouts with your buddies. Meetings should be regular and intentional to be effective. You can still "hang out", but a part of your meetings need to be focused on supporting your purity journey.

2. Boundaries / Rules – You need to setup boundaries and rules around your "triggery" areas. If you struggle on your tablet, you need some tablet boundaries. If you are attracted to a flirty girl at work, you probably need some work boundaries. The bigger the trigger, the bigger the boundaries need to be.

3. Accountability – This is a hybrid of meetings and boundaries. Your accountability might start with your Covenant Eyes accountability software, but your reports get sent to your Drill-Down people who have conversations with you. Self-accountability is not a real word. Accountability implies that you are giving an account to someone else about another area of your life. Schedule regular meetings with the people who can help you with accountability.

The hardest type of structure is any self-imposed, self-maintained, or self-motivated..

4. Self-Discipline – It's hard to grow at self-discipline if you have been extremely undisciplined in the past. You can't expect to go from 20% disciplined to 100% in a small amount of time. You grow in your discipline as you say no to worldly passions. Your ability to say no and not act in an unhealthy sexual way will grow as you pursue purity, heal on the inside, and work the other three structure areas.

THINK – SWIMMING LANES

Living with structure might be hard for you. Expect resistance and even rebellion to surface. You might be the type of person who doesn't like the idea of rules or boundaries. Maybe you don't want someone telling you what to do. Maybe you don't want another person to see your Internet history.

Structure provides a framework for proper building. Structure provides boundaries and guidelines for us to function and perform at our best. Structure allows us to walk in freedom. Structure helps us guard against acting out and missteps.

Lane dividers are provided to help a swimmer to do his best. They are not there to constrict or to prevent freedom. Lanes are an important structure to help the swimmers stay focused, be protected from other swimmers, and show swimmers where they can swim freely.

> **Day 11 Action Step:** Take a moment right now and talk to God about your attitude toward structure.

> Ask Him to help you see structure in a proper light.

> Ask Him to show you what the right structure is for your purity journey.

> If you have rebelled against structure, accountability, rules and boundaries, talk to Him about it. Confess to Him. Ask Him to turn your heart.

DAILY, WEEKLY & ONGOING STRUCTURE IDEAS

> **Day 11 Action Step:** Check any of the ideas below that you'd like to implement. Write your own in the margins (or in your notebook).

Daily

- A daily Bible reading prayer time
- Specifically praying to God about your recovery
- Daily checking in with a sponsor or accountability person
- Daily reading or listening to recovery material

Weekly

- A meeting with your support group
- A meeting with your counselor
- A meeting with your accountability partner

Ongoing

- Filters and accountability software for your computer, tablet, phone or other   device
- Boundaries for your TV, DVDs, movies, magazines and other media
- Boundaries for work, school and dating
- Hangouts with buddies who are encouraging and know some of your story
- Special conferences or meetings that will help train you in purity

DAY 12 – SEEK ACCOUNTABILITY

Accountability happens when you give an account for an area of your life. You have to be intentional about accountability. It will not find you. Set it up as part of your structure and find another person you can report to.

Accountability is about transparency. You are open and honest with someone on your support team about a key area.

Accountability goes to the deeper levels. Your buddies know the best. You have built trust with one another and you are able to drill-down with them into more sensitive areas.

WHERE DO I FIND AN ACCOUNTABILITY PARTNER?

Every accountability partner starts out as general support. Drill-down relationships emerge as you find people with whom you have good chemistry and good trust.

Start your search among these eight pools groups of people:

1. <u>Close friends</u> – Safe friends who are active in your life and know your story make the best accountability partners.

2. <u>Old friends</u> – They can be brought up to speed quickly and are another good option.

3. <u>Church small group members</u> – If you are doing Bible study with some good guys, you might be able to find someone with similar struggles. Christian men and women struggle too. They just haven't found someone safe to talk to about their struggles.

4. <u>Ministers</u> – It's good to have a relationship with a minister anyway. Ministers can be busy and have many they counsel with.

It's hard for a minister to be a regular accountability partner, but maybe your minister can help you get started.

5. <u>Counselors</u> – They are always solid options and confidential. Counselors can get expensive, but they will do a good job of getting you started.

6. <u>Support group members</u> – They are a great option! They can be an instant group of friends that will understand your struggles. Look there for peers, veterans and sponsors to be good accountability partners.

7. <u>Spouse</u> – Your spouse is a natural accountability partner for you, but he or she may have been damaged by your sexual struggles. As your marriage heals, your spouse will be able to help more. If you and your spouse are in a healthy place, give it a try. Make sure you don't load your spouse down with all of your accountability needs. Look for someone of the same gender to share the burden.

8. <u>Family members</u> - Family members are good general support, but sometimes it's hard for them to ask the tough questions. If you have a family member that can be safe and confidential, then go for it!

➤ **Day 12 Action Step:** Write down the people from your circles of relationships whom you think could make good accountability partners:

➤ Close friends –

➤ Old friends –

➢ Church small group members -

➢ Ministers –

➢ Counselors –

➢ Support Group Members -

➢ Spouse -

➢ Family Members -

FIVE ESSENTIALS FOR EVERY ACCOUNTABILITY RELATIONSHIP

1. Committed to the Process – You and your accountability partner have to be intentional. There needs to be a commitment on both parts. One person cannot run the process while the other one drags his feet.

2. Accountability – There has to be a part of the meeting where you are asked to account for something. If there is no accountability, it's simply a hangout, support group, fellowship or breakfast appointment.

3. Drill-Down – You have to go deeper in your relationship with others. Accountability partners need to know each other deeply. They need to come up with questions to ask one another. And they need to call B.S. when necessary.

4. **Supportive** – Accountability relationships are not places to get beat up, yelled at or shamed when you have a sexual slip. They need to be places where The Great Commandment is practiced.

"Teacher, which is the greatest commandment in the Law?"

Jesus replied: "'Love the Lord your God with all your heart and with all your soul and with all your mind.' This is the first and greatest commandment. And the second is like it: 'Love your neighbor as yourself.' Matthew 22:36-39

Love your brother or sister by supporting them in their sexual purity process. Lift them up. Pray for them. Encourage them. Carry one another's burdens. Grow your relationships into the deepest oasis of God's grace and love.

5. **Flexible** – You need to adjust to one another. Try different things in your meetings until you get it right. Adjust your meeting time until you find the right one. If the person is getting better in an area of accountability, go deeper. Ask a different question or move on to an area that needs more work. Raise your bottom lines when you need to. Bring in different questions when new struggles arise.

ACCOUNTABILITY JUMPSTARTS

At our PurityCoaching.com website, we offer a service called Accountability Jumpstarts. We are willing to be your accountability partner for 1, 2 or 3 months. Go to the "accountability" page on our site and check it out.

➤ **Day 12 Action Step:** Reach out to one or two people at the top of your list of potential accountability partners. Initiate. Make a phone call. Send an email or text. Test the waters and invite them to support you in a drill-down way.

➤ **Day 12 Action Step:** Contact our ministry if you have an immediate need for accountability. Use the coupon in the back of this book for a special discount.

DAY 13 – IDENTIFY YOUR TRIGGERS

A trigger is anything that sets you off emotionally. Triggers can be sexual, non-sexual, or environmental. Triggers can be internal feelings or external. Triggers can come from people, places, objects or feelings.

Some examples of triggers could be:

- A beautiful woman at the gym
- A sexually explicit scene in a movie
- A party you and your friends are attending
- A magazine on the rack at the grocery store
- A stressful work week
- A conflict with your spouse
- An old friend on Facebook you used to date
- Times you feel alone, bored, sad or lonely

Triggers by themselves are not sinful. Beautiful women, magazines and parties are a part of normal life. So is work, stress, conflict, feeling bored and feeling alone. You get in trouble with your triggers when you decide to deal with them in unhealthy, ungodly sexual ways.

You can see a pretty girl at the gym, recognize her beauty and move on. Or you can stare at her, approach her, follow her or fantasize about her later. Triggers happen. What you do with your triggers is where a good purity strategy will come in.

The first step in developing a good strategy is identifying your triggers.

IDENTIFY YOUR TRIGGERS

Spend some time in this next section identifying what types of people, places, things and feelings get your attention and set you off emotionally. Think about your past reactions and triggers that have led to slips.

What you're doing is learning to "check the nouns". Zero in on people, places or things that set you off and affect your sexual purity journey.

> **Day 13 Action Step:** In each section below, try to identify your triggers. Be as specific and as thorough as you wish.

PEOPLE TRIGGERS

Specific Names – These would be people whose names you know. They could be people at work, school or church. They could be movie, TV or porn stars. They could be old crushes, boyfriends or girlfriends.

> Write your specific people triggers below.

Types of People – You don't know these people, but you like their body type, the way they dress, the way they act, etc. You could be as specific as "blonde-hair, blue-eyed girls". Or more general like "cheerleaders", "trashy" or "well-dressed".

> Write your types of people triggers below.

PLACE TRIGGERS

Think about the places you go that are "triggery" for you and cause you to think in a sexual manner. They might be pools, beaches or parties. They might be airports or places you have traveled solely to hook up with others. Think about places you pass by while you are on the road that might cause you to think sexually. Specific websites you turn to for sexual kicks are also places full of triggers (think social media, chat rooms and image search sites).

> Write down your place triggers in the space below.

THING TRIGGERS

You are also triggered by things. Think about media outlets like magazines, newspaper circulars, and catalogues. Think about your computer or your phone. Think about clothing fetishes you have. Think about anything lying around the house that you can go to for sexual kicks.

> Write your thing triggers below.

FEELINGS TRIGGERS

You might not have thought about being triggered by your own feelings, but they are a very common source. We can be triggered when we are bored, hungry, angry, lonely, tired, sick, sad or stressed. We can also be triggered when we are happy and excited.

➢ Write down the feelings that most often trigger you to think in a sexual direction.

➢ **Day 13 Action Step:** Go back to each of the trigger sections and circle your TOP THREE. Now rank them. These are the triggers you need to give the most attention to in your purity strategy.

DAY 14 – IDENTIFY YOUR FEELINGS AND DESIRES

Sexual purity and sexual impurity flow from the deepest levels of your heart. If you want to understand your struggles, you have to go below the surface. Unhealthy sexual behaviors are an indicator that something is not healthy underneath. If you're doing well on your sexual purity journey, you probably have some good things going on inside of you.

Exploring the deep levels is one of the best purity jumpstart exercises you can do. This is advanced stuff, so if it doesn't make sense right away, that's okay. Mark the chapter and come back to it later.

You already looked at the first sublevel yesterday – triggers. Today you'll explore two more areas.

Sublevel #1 - Triggers. What people, places, things and feelings set you off and get you thinking in a sexual direction?

Sublevel #2 – Feelings. What emotions are attached to your triggers?

Sublevel #3 – Desires. What God-given needs are your seeking to be filled?

TRIGGERS

⇩

set off

FEELINGS

⇩

which are attached to

DESIRES

FEELINGS

A few words about feelings…

1. **It's OK to Feel -** Feelings are not for "sissies", weak people, or girls only. They are God-given and felt by all. Great men and women in the Bible felt and wrote about their feelings. Jesus felt and found healthy ways to express His feelings.

    The Book of Psalms is a great place to learn about feelings and connecting with God about your feelings. It may surprise you how honest some of the psalmists were about their feelings.

2. **Practice Getting Your Feelings Out –** Find a way to work through feelings, especially when you are having a difficult time emotionally. Don't hold your feelings in. Don't think they will go away. If you are consumed with your thoughts and they are taking up real estate in your heart, go the next step.

    - Write them out in a journal or notebook.

    - Talk them out with a counselor.

    - Express them to your support group.

    - Disclose them to a close friend.

3. **Get Ready to Feel More –** When you stop looking at porn, you will start feeling more. Porn provides an emotional counterfeit. Porn will excite you and jolt your brain chemicals tremendously, but it really numbs you and limits your true range of emotions. When you get healthy, you will feel more. The highs will be higher and the lows will be lower. You don't have to be afraid of the lows or the increase of negative emotions if you have God in your life. The best thing is that you will experience a satisfaction and contentment

that porn could never deliver. As you walk away from porn and sexual impurity, you take steps toward maturing emotionally.

> **Day 14 Action Step:** Pick up a notebook or journal today so you can start recording and processing the deeper stuff.

FOUR "WORK OUT YOUR FEELINGS" EXERCISES

Exercise #1: Start asking yourself, "What am I feeling underneath?" and write it down. Get as detailed as you can about where you are emotionally.

Exercise #2: If you have a slip, ask the trigger question, then ask the feeling question. What was triggering you? What were your feeling?

Exercise #3: Give it a number. How intense was your feeling? Rate your feelings from 1-10 with 10 being the most intense. How you treat an 8 or 9 is different from a 2 or a 3.

Exercise #4: Sometimes you have heavy emotional patches. They may last a few hours or several days. Work them out in your notebook or with a friend, especially if you can't seem to shake them.

SEVEN GOD-GIVEN DESIRES

I'm grateful to Mark and Debra Laaser for their book, *The Seven Desires of Every Heart*. In this book, they talk about seven universal, God-given desires everyone has. They are:

1. <u>To Be Heard and Understood</u> – You want people to listen to you and not blow you off. You want others to know your point of view, your needs and your concerns.

2. <u>To Be Affirmed</u> – You want what you do on the outside (accomplishments, deeds, work, etc.) to be recognized.

3. <u>To Be Blessed</u> – You want who you are on the inside to be recognized.

4. <u>To Be Safe</u> – You want to feel secure and protected.

5. <u>To Be Touched</u> – You want physical connection with others. Sexual touch and non-sexual touch.

6. <u>To Be Chosen</u> – You want to be important to someone else.

7. <u>To Be Included</u> – You want to be part of a larger team.

Read the book when you get a chance, especially if you are trying to understand the deeper things that drive you.

As you get better at identifying your triggers and feelings, look also for your desires. Ask yourself, "What God-given desire am I looking to fulfill?"

> **Day 14 Action Step:** Go back to the Seven Desires list. Which 1 or 2 desires are the biggest needs for you?

> Q: What connections do you see between your desires and your sexual struggles?

Laser, Mark and Laaser, Debra. *The Seven Desires of Every Heart.* Zondervan, 2008. Print.

DAY 15 – BUILD YOUR SPIRITUAL LIFE

You're never going to heal from your sexual struggles until you get your spiritual life figured out.

This book has exposed you to the 4 S's: Support, Structure, Strategy and Spiritual Life. All are important for your sexual purity journey. You will need to have active plans for building each of them.

How many of the 4 S's are you working? Which one do you most often neglect? For many, it is the spiritual life. Today's lesson will give you some tips on growing your spiritual life the right way.

You have a spiritual part of your life just like you have physical, emotional, relational, mental and sexual parts. A part of you wants to connect with God. You were created by God and built for connections with Him.

You were designed first, for a **vertical** connection. To get strong spiritually you need to cultivate your relationship with God. You do this through prayer, reading the Bible, serving and worshipping.

Another part of your spiritual life is **horizontal**. This is where you connect with others who love God. You build upon your week opportunities to worship as a group, serve others, attend small group Bible study, and hang out with those who seek God. The Bible talks over and over about our need for "one another." You need to build up your horizontal connections in order to be strong spiritually.

> ➤ **Day 15 Action Step:** Evaluate how your vertical connections are doing.

➢ **Day 15 Action Step:** Evaluate how your horizontal connections are doing.

MAKE SURE YOU'RE CONNECTED SPIRITUALLY TO GOD

You have the capacity to connect with God because of your spiritual nature, but it's not automatic. The Bible is clear that the entryway to God is through a personal relationship with Jesus. Make sure you know what that means. There's an incredible amount of power for your purity journey that comes from your connection with God.

There's a special chapter in the Appendix (and in the videos) called *Salvation*. It will help you understand more about your relationship with God.

> "For God so loved the world that he gave his one and only Son, that whoever believes in him shall not perish but have eternal life." John 3:16

> "Jesus answered, 'I am the way and the truth and the life. No one comes to the Father except through me.'"
> John 14:6

VERTICAL CONNECTION TIPS

1. <u>Regular place and time</u> – Make your time with God a part of the rhythm of your day. Commit to it. Figure out a good place and time you can schedule your appointments with God. Is your better time early in the morning, during your commute to work, at your desk at work, during your lunch break or at night?

2. <u>Pray in a different way</u> – Practice being open and honest with God. Forget formal. Speak from your heart. Talk with God about what you're struggling with, triggered by, feeling or desiring. Talk to Him about the good things that are happening too. Ask Him to help you where your heart is at.

3. <u>Read purity passages first</u> – A good way to strengthen your sexual purity journey is to focus on passages that relate to sexual purity and the larger purity process. Here are few of my favorite to get your started.

   - I Corinthians 6:12-20
   - I Thessalonians 4:1-12
   - Romans 8
   - Galatians 5
   - Proverbs 5, 6 or 7

4. <u>Shoot for meaningful connections</u> – It's more important for you to have a genuine connection with God, rather than just checking a box. Who cares if you met with God seven times this week if they weren't meaningful? Meaningful connections are heart-to-heart. You reach God's direction and He reaches back to you with His presence and His Word. A good accountability question is "What meaningful connections have you made with God during this past week?"

HORIZONTAL CONNECTION TIPS

1. <u>View these as just as important as the vertical</u> – You may be a loner and an introvert, but you need connections with others. You need spiritual people to teach you and help you. You need heart-to-heart connections with spiritual people. You and God going through life alone is not the plan laid out in God's Word.

2. Regular place and time – You need to find your daily and weekly rhythm for connecting with others too. Your routine may be a daily phone call or weekly Bible study meeting. Certainly worshipping with others in a local church is an easy way to build your spiritual life. Figure out what you need to schedule each week to keep your horizontal connections in front of you.

3. Stretching is normal – Growing your spiritual relationships with others may be uncomfortable at first, especially if you've been alone spiritually. Be courageous. Keep working on it. As you find your rhythm it will get easier.

4. Initiate, invite, ask – You probably need to be the one to reach out, sign up, and ask questions. Don't wait for others to ask you. Your purity journey is important to you and so is your spiritual journey. Initiate the connections and follow through with your action plan. If you don't know where the best churches are or small group meetings with spiritual people, do the research or ask for referrals.

➢ **Day 15 Action Step:** What adjustments do you need to make with your vertical connection?

➢ **Day 15 Action Step:** What adjustments do you need to make with your horizontal connections?

DAY 16 – TAKE SIN SERIOUSLY

Get a bigger picture of sin. Get a bigger picture of grace.

Today and tomorrow focus on spiritual thinking and a correct understanding of sin and grace. These won't be full treatments of either subject. This is a jumpstart. You need to get your thinking moving in this direction. Some definitions might be helpful as you start:

SIN = Rebellion against God and His standards. Sin can happen in your heart, in your mind, and certainly with your actions. You can sin against God, others and yourself.

As a sexual struggler, it is important to accept your sinful condition, own it (take responsibility) and turn to Jesus as the solution to your sins.

GRACE = The free, unmerited favor of God. God's love for you is unconditional. His ultimate display of love for you is through Jesus' death on the cross. Grace is shown to you by God. He has paid for the sins of the world knowing that you will still sin. And even though He knows you are a sinner, He still pursues a relationship with you. You will continue to struggle and fail on your sexual journey, but this will never nullify the grace of God.

As a sexual struggler it is important for you to believe God's grace, accept it, and walk in it.

HOW'S YOUR TIRE PRESSURE?

If you neglect sin or grace, your sexual purity journey will be lopsided. Like the air pressure in your car's tires, you need to have to the proper amount of PSI; you don't want it be overinflated or underinflated.

Sin Overinflated, Grace Underinflated – Your sins are all you see. You see your life and behaviors and think "failure." You have no room for God's grace. You have trouble experiencing the love, mercy, hope, peace and joy that God has called you to. You have trouble hanging around others who model God's love and grace. You see the reason Jesus died, but you do not see the glorious result.

Grace Overinflated, Sin Underinflated - Sin is either non-existent to you, or part of your vocabulary. You talk about love, grace, mercy, hope, and peace all of the time. You talk about second, third and fourth chances. Repentance, consequences and punishment are not a part of your vocabulary. You believe in the death of Jesus, but all you focus on is on the end result.

Sin And Grace Both Underinflated – You have a hard time taking responsibility for your struggles and you have no hope. You may be a blamer. You blame everyone else for your problems. You are fatalistic. You seem doomed about your addiction and your struggling existence.

Balanced Understanding of Sin and Grace – You are like the Apostle Paul who understood well the death of Jesus and the freedom from bondage His death provided. You struggle, you trip up, but your spiritual focus is not deterred. You hold tightly onto God's grace over you. You reach for His promises and let His Word guide your thinking and heart.

SIN BASICS

1. You have sin.
2. Your sin has consequences and leads you down the path of death and destruction.
3. Your sin is worse than you realize.
4. Jesus died for your sins to take them away.
5. Your sin has been conquered once and for all through Christ's death.
6. Your sin still has effects in your heart that affect your purity journey.

Here are a few exercises to get you to think and explore what the Bible says about sin.

THE PROGRESSION AND CONSEQUENCES OF SIN

➢ **Day 16 Action Step:** Get a Bible and read Romans 1:18-32. What are the consequences of sin? How does sin erode you?

➢ How do you see sin in this passage getting progressively worse?

Romans 1 is a sad chapter to read. It's heavy. It shows the progression of sin and its downward spiral. Unchecked and undealt with, your sin will continue to multiply, spin out of control and take you to places you never wished to go. You may have already visited some of those places. Guaranteed... If you don't get honest with your sin and deal with it, you will continue to deteriorate spiritually.

➢ In what ways have you seen your own sexual sins get progressively worse (either in the past or in the present)?

OWNING IT, REALIZING HOW BAD IT IS

> **Day 16 Action Step:** Read the passage below where Paul called himself the "worst of sinners" ("chief of sinners" in KJV).

Here is a trustworthy saying that deserves full acceptance: Christ Jesus came into the world to save sinners—of whom I am the worst. But for that very reason I was shown mercy so that in me, the worst of sinners, Christ Jesus might display his immense patience as an example for those who would believe in him and receive eternal life. I Timothy 1:15-16

> What do you think Paul was trying to communicate to his readers when he said this?

It seems absurd that the Apostle Paul would consider himself the worst of sinners. Paul was a super-Christian, if there ever was one. He was the first century's most successful missionary. He wrote thirteen of the books of the New Testament, yet he struggled with his sin. He was aware that his sinful nature was at war with his godly nature.

Paul never forgot where he came from - He persecuted the church. He killed Christians. He was extremely religious and zealous on the outside, but evil on the inside. Paul never forgot what Jesus rescued him from.

> Are you owning (taking responsibility for) your sexual sins? How do you know?

> When you don't own your own sexual sins, you blame others and make excuses. What are some ways you have shifted the blame and made excuses for your own actions?

Paul saw his sin more clearly as he saw God's grace more clearly - Jesus appeared to Paul in Acts 9 and turned the light switch on. Jesus changed his life in a powerful encounter. Paul's awakening helped him see both his sin and God's grace more clearly.

> *But where sin increased, grace increased all the more, so that, just as sin reigned in death, so also grace might reign through righteousness to bring eternal life through Jesus Christ our Lord. Romans 5:20-21*

God does not leave you in your sinful state. He wants you to understand sin and its effects on your life, but He follows up with hope, mercy and grace. Tomorrow's focus is on grace. It's a very important chapter. We must have a balanced understanding of grace as well.

DAY 17 – TAKE GRACE SERIOUSLY

Get a bigger picture of sin. Get a bigger picture of grace.

GRACE = The free, unmerited favor of God. God's love for you is unconditional. His ultimate display of love for you is through Jesus' death on the cross. Grace is shown to you by God. He has paid for the sins of the world knowing that you will still sin. And even though He knows you are a sinner, He still pursues a relationship with you. You will continue to struggle and fail on your sexual purity journey, but this will never nullify the grace of God.

As a sexual struggler it is important for you to believe God's grace, accept it, and walk in it.

God's love for you is huge. He knows you inside and out. He knew you before you were born, as you were born, as you grew up, as you made mistakes, and as your sexual struggles evolved. God knows you now. God is intimately acquainted with everything about you.

As a sexual struggler, it's scary to think about sharing your struggles with someone else. You worry about what they will think of you. You worry about how they will react and treat you. You worry about hurting them and having changes within your friendships. These problems could happen with some of your friends, but they will never happen with God. He already knows you, loves you, and is safe to turn to.

> ➤ **Day 17 Action Step:** Read this amazing grace verse below:

> *"But God demonstrates his own love for us in this: While we were still sinners, Christ died for us." Romans 5:8*

> ➤ How is this verse an encouragement to you on your sexual purity journey?

A requirement for every sexual struggler should be to read Romans 8. If you want to see a grace-filled chapter, this is it. In my sexual purity groups, I ask every guy to go here. Every sexual struggler I have worked with has times where he suffers with shame and becomes overwhelmed by his sins and his failures. Frustrations can morph into you "beating yourself up". It is a form of self-hatred. God never does this. He knows your sin and still offers His grace and unconditional love for you.

Romans 8 can help you not be so hard on yourself. Learn to see yourself how God sees you. This chapter will help.

➢ **Day 17 Action Step:** Get a Bible. Find Romans 8. And do a small bible study. The questions below will guide you through this wonderful, grace-filled scripture.

Verses 1 & 2 - How do these verses encourage you?

Verses 9, 10 & 11 - If you belong to Christ, what do these verses say about your sins?

Who is living in you? What difference does that make on your sexual purity journey?

<u>Verses 14 to 17</u> - *Abba* means *daddy* in Hebrew. In addition to God being your daddy, what other relationship terms does this passage use?

<u>Verses 26 & 28</u> - How are these verses an encouragement to you with your sexual struggles?

<u>Verses 31 to 38</u> - This is a masterful, beautiful encouraging passage! How does this help you on your sexual purity journey?

GUILT VS SHAME

Different authors and ministers have different takes on shame. Some see there being good shame and bad shame. Some see shame completely in a negative light. I see...

GUILT - You are guilty of breaking God's laws. This is sin. You are responsible. You have done it. You have no excuse. Guilty as charged. Guilt is over the things that you have done and thought in your heart. Ultimately, sin comes from the heart. All mankind is guilty of sin.

SHAME - This is different from guilt. Guilt's message is "You are guilty." Shame's message is "You are worthless". Shame doesn't focus on your actions. It focuses on your insides and calls them bad. You believe you are a bad person. You believe what you have done is who you are. You see yourself as worthless, a loser, a lost cause or hopeless. Shame talks you into believing that you are no good and that it might have been better if you had not been born.

Do any of these messages seem like they would have come from God? No!

Is this what God thinks of you? No!

I have a friend who calls them "shame lies". I like that. Shame lies tell us that we are no good.

Shame is more than just bad self-esteem. Shame lies are the whispers of the Enemy in your ears. Shame is your sinful nature talking to you, putting you down, putting down God, and making you think you are not worthy of God's love. Your Enemy, the Devil, wins the victory every time you believe shame lies.

A great part of the sexual purity journey is when God brings His truth to your shame lies. The only way you are going to cut through the core of your inward beliefs is by injecting the truth of the Word of God. That's why you spent so much time today in Romans 8.

Other Bible passages that will help you combat shame lies:

- Jeremiah 1
- Psalm 139
- Ephesians 1

DAY 18 – GO BACKWARD

Your past, present and future are all important to your purity journey.

Past – What influences of the past have helped or hurt your purity journey? What are the roots of your struggles?

Present – What decisions are you making now that are helping our hurting your purity journey?

Future – Where are you headed? What's your purity vision? What larger purity goals are you shooting for?

Most of the 21-Day Purity Jumpstart focuses on the present. Today you'll look back at the past. Tomorrow, you'll look forward to the future.

WHAT DO YOU MEAN, LOOK BACKWARD?

Your sexual struggles came from somewhere. To better understand them you have look at the past to uncover the roots. What people influenced you? What environments influenced you? What affect did your peers have on you? What about traumatic events? And how did the people around you talk about sexuality? It's worth your time to reflect and look for insights from your past.

No one is the product of perfect parents, perfect environments, perfect churches, or perfect relationships. There are many parts of your past that have brought damage. Sometimes the wounding has a significant impact on your ability to move forward. You will need God to help you heal from wounds of the past.

AREAS TO CONSIDER WHEN WORKING BACKWARD

- Family atmosphere
- Spiritual atmosphere
- Peer atmosphere

- Early exposure to pornography
- Girlfriends/boyfriends and sexual history
- Wounds, broken relationships
- Triggers and stressors that lead to acting out
- Shame, anger and other emotions that keep you in the past

> **Day 18 Action Step:** Start with one area, MEDIA. Think about each category. How did each one influence your thoughts about sex? What lessons did you learn from each area about sex and how to treat the opposite sex?

The more thought you can give to this action step, the more insights you will have.

TV –

Movies –

Concerts –

Radio –

Internet –

Magazines –

<u>Newspapers</u> –

<u>Catalogues</u> –

<u>Other Media</u> –

You can do this backward exercise with any area of your past.

Backward is where a lot of healing and insight takes place. You learn a lot about why you struggle with sexual purity. You learn to identify your triggers. You learn to listen to your heart, emotions and needs. You have to go backward to work on the pain.

When working backward, it's important to have wise people around you. Spending time in the counselor's office, the pastor's office and support groups will help you unpack your past and work through it. Seek God's healing for wounds and sore spots that are uncovered.

If you need some help with going backward, send me an email at <u>jeff@puritycoaching.com</u>. I'd be glad to help.

DAY 19 – GO FORWARD

Keep going forward. Don't get side tracked. Don't get stuck in the past. Don't plateau. Don't set the gear into neutral.

You can get stuck in your purity journey when you…

- Don't deal with your wounds and find God's healing.
- Don't deal with setbacks, slips and relapses very well.
- Go back into isolation.
- Have success and think you've arrived.
- Your short-term motivations are exhausted.

MOTIVATIONS

Motivations drive your commitment to purity. Motivations fuel your efforts to be sexually pure.

> **Day 19 Action Step:** What are your motivations for being sexual pure? See if you can write out 7 of them.

1.

2.

3.

4.

5

6.

7.

Your motivations will change as you go through recovery. Hopefully, they will deepen, and cause you to become more focused on God than on yourself.

Some motivations are short-termed and rather short-sighted. "I want my spouse to stop being angry with me" or "I want to be able get the restrictions off of my computer" are things that motivate you, but do not complete the bigger picture. They have more to do with your comfort level than they do being healthy sexually.

Bigger picture motivations might be "I want to have a healthy relationship with my spouse" or "I want to be able to use my computer as a productive tool and not a way to get my sexual fix."

Your motivations will help you see where your focus is, in the short-term or the long-term. It's not wrong to have short-term motivations, but if you are looking to be sexually pure for the long haul, you will need to see the big picture.

THINK ABOUT GOD'S BIGGER PICTURE OF PURITY

Let these scriptures challenge you and help you see God's bigger idea of purity:

> "But among you there must <u>not be even a hint of sexual immorality, or of any kind of impurity,</u> or of greed, because these are improper for God's holy people." *Ephesians 5:3*

> "Religion that God our Father accepts as pure and faultless is this: to look after orphans and widows in their distress <u>and to keep oneself from being polluted by the world.</u>" *James 1:27*

You may start having some success on your purity journey by having a consistent string of good days. Celebrate it! Thank God for it. Share it with your support team. But don't think that you have arrived. Don't shift into maintenance mode. There is no neutral gear in sexual purity. You must always be engaged, either in reverse or in drive.

Here's another good passage reminding you to keep moving forward:

"Not that I have already obtained all this, or have already arrived at my goal, but I press on to take hold of that for which Christ Jesus took hold of me. Brothers and sisters, I do not consider myself yet to have taken hold of it. But one thing I do: Forgetting what is behind and straining toward what is ahead, I press on toward the goal to win the prize for which God has called me heavenward in Christ Jesus." Philippians 3:12-14

HELP OTHERS

There are times on your sexual purity journey when you have to focus on yourself. If you are in a crisis or have been deeply wounded, you probably shouldn't be trying to help others. You need to work on you for a while. As you move forward on your journey, you will be put in a position to help others.

When you help others, your focus will shift off of yourself. This is a great offensive strategy. Sexual sin is selfish. You need to practice turning your attention to others as much as possible. Turn outward instead of inward.

Helping others starts with **sharing part of your story**. It is helpful for strugglers to know there are other strugglers. **Tell them your work-in-progress story.** You have not arrived. You are not a purity expert. You are a fellow struggler who is getting healthy. Frame it that way. Help others who are broken through your own brokenness. Share with others how God is helping you.

> ➢ **Day 19 Action Step:** If you were sharing your "work in progress" story with someone who just started their recovery, what key points would you mention?

The more you move forward with success in your purity journey, the more you will be able to help others.

DAY 20 – COMMITMENT AND RECOMMITMENT

Keep making commitments and recommitments.

Your sexual purity journey is a <u>journey</u>. No journey that's worthwhile is easy. As you have probably discovered, there are a lot of ups and downs. There are a lot of successes and failures. It can seem like there are more downs, failures, frustrations, pain and suffering, and maybe at certain points on your journey there are. That's normal.

- It's normal for you to struggle.
- It's normal for you to want to quit at times.
- It's normal for you to feel like you've tried everything to succeed (when really you haven't).
- It's normal to have moments and days where you lose hope.

The material from Day 19 is so important to consider as you make your commitments. Big picture motivations and big picture visions will help you frame your commitments in the right way. If your commitment is short-sighted, your success or failure will be short-sighted. If you make a commitment to yourself to not look at porn for 30 days, and you stumble, what does that say about your purity journey? Is it a failure? Hardly. A porn slip is a setback and could require major attention. But in light of the much bigger process you are going through, your porn slip is just a small bump on the much bigger purity journey.

KEEP MAKING COMMITMENTS

When you commit to yourself, others and to God, you are showing your determination and motivation. Of course, you could be making a commitment only to please someone else. But it's safe to assume if you have gotten this far in the book, you want to succeed in purity for yourself.

Here are some tips about commitments:

1. <u>Commit first to the big picture</u> – Make a commitment to shoot for God's big picture of purity.

2. <u>Get heavy support for the "no fly zone" commitments</u> – There are behaviors you need to stop and never go back to again. If you are committing adultery, hooking up with others, or doing illegal sexual activities you absolutely need to stop. Make a commitment to stop now, and get some serious support. Some behaviors have consequences that are severe. Your commitment needs to be as equally severe.

3. <u>Make commitments that are in your range</u> – If you have been looking at porn and masturbating every day, it's tough to make and keep a 30-day commitment. Of course you need a goal to aim for, but why not break it up in smaller chunks. Work with your support team on this. You might need to make commitments that are moment-by-moment or one day at a time. Tailor your commitments and your support in a way that helps you build momentum.

4. <u>Make commitments that can be tracked</u> – You want to be able to track your success or failures. Commitments to love God more, be more serious about your purity or do better at night are not specific enough. They can't be tracked very well. Commitments need action steps that can be accomplished.

5. <u>Make commitments known to your support team</u> – You need your support team for this journey. Make sure to involve them.

6. <u>Seek God's strength for your commitments</u> – It's easy to make a commitment and have early success on your own strength, but your willpower and determination will not fuel you for the long haul. Seek God every day for the strength you need to keep your commitments.

KEEP MAKING RECOMMITMENTS

When you struggle in your commitments or have neglected them, you need to make a recommitment. Recommitments are fresh starts. They are a refocusing of your intent and efforts. Recommitments must happen in your purity journey.

Spiritually, recommitments mean repentance. You repent when you make a U-turn. You realize that you are no longer going in God's direction and you need to turn around and head in the right direction. When you repent, you must acknowledge your sin, turn from it and seek God's face.

Repentance is not a one-time event. It is an ongoing mindset. You can make a very distinct reversal of your direction, but you must also walk in it. You can repent of your immoral actions, but you also make daily choices to continue in that state of repentance.

Day 9 has some great tips on how to navigate slips and relapses. Make sure you go back to that day. Review your action steps on how to bounce back effectively. Also, go back and watch the video for Day 9.

> **Day 20 Action Step:** What commitment(s) or recommitment(s) do you need to make? Write them in the space below.

DAY 21 – MILESTONES

Milestones are motivating. When you reach a milestone in your sexual purity journey it's exhilarating! Whether, it's coming out of isolation, stopping an adulterous relationship, not looking at porn for 30 days, not masturbating, visiting a counselor for the first time, or attending a support group for the first time, you will be pumped up once your reach it.

The sexual purity journey is a marathon. It's a long process. You will have many ups and downs. You will have good, bad and ugly days. Everyone does. No one takes a 3-week course on purity and becomes a master. And really, no one goes 5, 10, or 20 years without having struggles and hard patches. But if you are focused and your heart is set on purity, you will reach some great milestones.

Take some time now to recognize milestones in your purity journey you've already hit. They don't have to be humongous; they just need to be significant.

> **Day 21 Action Step** – Write down the milestones you've achieved already in your sexual purity journey. Write down victories and high points from your past.

CHART YOUR PROGRESS IN A BETTER WAY

Don't forget, your purity journey is not just about your behaviors. Your purity journey is a total transformation. You are seeking to make progress emotionally, relationally, spiritually, sexually, mentally, and physically.

> **Day 21 Action Step:** Expand the way you chart your purity progress. What progress have you made in each of these areas?

Emotional (feelings, beliefs, dreams, reflections of your heart, desires) –

Relational (the way you relate with others) -

Spiritual (connecting with God and others who love God) -

Sexual (how you understand and express your *maleness* or *femaleness* -

Mental (education, understanding, reflection, critical thinking) -

Physical (behavioral, self-care, nutrition, exercise, medications, wellness) -

THREE BIG MILESTONES

I want to highlight three big purity milestones: lust, objectification and masturbation. I want to give you some tips on how to reach these milestones. Please understand, when I call these milestones, it doesn't mean you will never again lust, objectify or masturbate. The milestones you will achieve will not be behavior milestones, but instead not-being-controlled-by-my-behavior milestones.

When I was deep in my sexual sin, lust, objectification and masturbation were everyday occurrences. I had no defense, no offense, no support team, no structure, and no real spiritual life. I desperately needed a system to help me get control of my life. I hope in these last 3 weeks of the 21-Day Purity Jumpstart you have an understanding of what a good system looks like.

On your purity journey, don't make stopping lust, objectification and masturbation your targets. These are behaviors. Target the heart instead. The proper way to stop a behavior is to work on what is driving the behavior, the heart flow. Seek God's help, the help of godly people, and work the system I've been teaching you. God's Spirit brings healing from the inside out.

MILESTONE: STOPPING LUST

There's probably no other basic struggle in your sexual purity journey than besides lust. Lust is when you switch over from desiring those things you fantasize about often to how you should go about getting what you have desired.

Remember the battle for lust is in the heart. This is God's territory to change your heart. You control where you look, what you meditate on, who you hang out with and where you hang out at. So a large part of getting victory over lust requires you to work on everything you can control and seek help from God and others on the things you can't control.

Cut or Minimize the Sources

"Flee sexual immorality." I Cor. 6:18
"It is God's will that you should… avoid sexual immorality." I Thess. 4:3

Running away is a great purity principle. You need to stay far away from people, places and things that are tough for you. You can't be a hermit or a monk and shut off completely from life. Stay away from people, places and things that encourage you to lust. Remember to check your nouns.

"If your right hand causes you to stumble, cut it off." Matt. 5:30

Be serious about stumbling blocks. Cut them off and go cold turkey. Sacrifice for the sake of your purity.

Get Help from Others

"Learn how to control your own body" I Thess. 4:4
"Therefore confess your sins to each other and pray for each other so that you may be healed." James 5:16

This is where you tap into your support team. Get connected with a support group, an accountability partner and a counselor. Share your struggles with them. Talk with them about what triggers you and what you continually lust over.

Lean Hard on God for What You Can't Control

"The life I now live in the body, I live by faith in the Son of God" (Gal. 2:20)

You can control some of the sources that tempt you. You can control whether you talk to your support team about your struggles. You can't control who sits in front of you at church, the waitress you get at the restaurant, or the people at the department store who are dressed inappropriately. This is where you have to press into God. Put the battle in His hands. Ask Him to come alongside you and help you. Ask Him to fill your heart with love for others instead of lust.

Replace Lust with Love

> *"We ought always to thank God for you, brothers and sisters, and rightly so, because your faith is growing more and more, and the love all of you have for one another is increasing." II Thess. 1:3*

The Holy Spirit has given you a love for your brothers and sisters, but you've let lust overpower it and corrupt your love. Love turned into lust. You need God's Holy Spirit to fill you with His love once again.

Something practical you can control is finding ways to love and serve. Give, volunteer, and help others. Learn about the needs of another and watch the Spirit of God resurrect the love in your heart. You can't lust and love at the same time.

The deepest love comes from God Himself. Another thing you can control is making time to connect with God, soak in His love, and fill up on it.

> ➤ **Big Milestone Action Step:** Write your own action steps for your lust struggles? What do you need to adjust? What do you need to work on? What's your action plan?

MILESTONE: STOPPING OBJECTIFICATION

Objectification is when you look at others as objects instead of real people. You dehumanize them. You use them for your sexual gratification. You selfishly take them and bend them to your fantasies.

Finding victory from objectifying doesn't come easy. You have a lot of practice objectifying. You have been taught by peers, family members, TV, movies and music to objectify.

The same principles for stopping lust apply to objectification:

- Cut or minimize sources
- Get help from others
- Lean hard on God for what you can't control
- Replace objectification with love

There are two other tips that will help you with objectification:

Adopt a Saying that Helps You Think Straight

I'm not a fan of the word *mantra*, but you need a range of things you can say to yourself to help you focus on a woman as a real person instead of an object for your visual pleasure.

- *"She's a real girl."*
- *"Not for me"*
- *"She's not my wife."*
- *"She's a real person."*
- *"She's somebody's daughter, wife or mother."*
- *"Alright, Jeff. Keep your eyes moving!"*

Find one or two sayings that work for you. Work on humanizing the person you're looking at.

Turn to Your Accountability Buddies

Any time you bring your sexual struggle into the light and involve another person, you will become more serious about stopping objectification. Your accountability buddies can help you design the right set of questions to help you with objectification. Try these questions:

- "Who are the people you are objectifying?"
- "What's going on in your heart when you see them?"
- "What needs to change?"

➤ **Big Milestone Action Step:** Write out 3 or 4 sayings that will be helpful to you in moving your thinking along when you start to objectify.

➤ Objectification flows from your heart and mind. How can you work on your heart to get better about valuing and loving people?

MILESTONE: STOPPING MASTURBATION

One of the sexual purity milestones you want to work on is stopping masturbation. You've tried, right? Probably 1000 times, and maybe for months at a time, but you keep going back to it.

To work on masturbation, keep applying the same principles for lust and objectification.

- Cut or minimize sources
- Get help from others
- Lean hard on God for what you can't control
- Replace lust with love
- Adopt a saying that will help you think straight
- Turn to your accountability buddies

Add these two:

Explore What's Going on Underneath the Surface

It might help you to know that masturbation is not the issue. There are reasons you masturbate.

It feels good – The brain chemicals go haywire when you masturbate. The "feel good" juices, bonding juices, and numbing juices all get fired up when you have an orgasm.

You are medicating – You have deeper needs, desires and wounds underneath. Masturbating numbs you and makes the deeper issues disappear temporarily

You are conditioned to it – If you do something 1000 times, it becomes a pretty big habit. It becomes a regular part of our life and is hard to break.

You have deeper desires that are not satisfied – Your deepest desires don't find a fix with masturbation. They just go away for a moment. But once it comes back, your reaction is to go back to your faithful comforter of masturbation.

<u>The shame cycle repeats itself</u> – In marriage, sex and orgasms are wonderful. They draw you and your spouse closer together. Outside of marriage they are great for a moment, but are followed by shame.

Get Up, Get Moving

The quickest thing that will help you with your masturbation struggles is to physically get up and leave your location. Go downstairs. Go to a different room. Go outside. Go to the gym. When you get moving, you start to turn the wheels in a different direction.

Getting up and getting moving will give you enough of a break from your struggle to do something from your offensive purity strategy. This will give you time to phone a friend from your support team, call on God and reach out in a different direction.

> **Big Milestone Action Step:** When you masturbate, what do you think you are medicating?

> Write out the strategy you need to employ the next time you feel like you want to masturbate.

POST 21 PURITY

Congratulations on making it to the end! For me, it feels good to get to the end of any workbook and resource. I'm already excited about the progress you will make past 21 days.

WHAT'S THE NEXT STEP FOR YOU?

If this is your first read through the 21-Day Purity Jumpstart, great. You probably read it fast or skimmed through some of the action points. I would encourage you to go through the book again a little slower. If the areas you skimmed are important to you, read over them again. A resource like this will better aid you the more you read it.

Perhaps the videos or audio would be a help to you. You can find those on our website www.puritycoaching.com.

Perhaps you'd like some one-on-one help with purity coaching or accountability. You can find that on our website, or by emailing me jeff@puritycoaching.com.

WHAT'S THE NEXT RESOURCE FOR YOU?

It's always good to have the next resource lined up as you approach the end of one. What's your next book? Podcast? Training conference? Attend a men's or women's conference?

LEARN THE BASICS WELL

It's not only important to make sure you have a handle on the 101 purity principles, but also that you are focused on mastering them. The bare bone principles I've presented in this material are the 4 S's. But I have also given you 21 big purity topics in this book. Do you feel like you have understood them enough to create a workable plan?

When you learn the basics, you can branch out and do amazing things. You can adapt, modify and improvise. If you have the basics down, it won't matter what life throws at you because you will have a core understanding of sexual purity that will assist you.

UPCOMING RESOURCES

I have several other resources in the works. Here's what's coming up:
<u>21-Day Accountability Jumpstart</u> – This is a three week journey to help you understand accountability. What is it? How do you find an accountability partner? How do you do accountability effectively? And how do you stay in it for the long haul?

<u>21-Day Support Group Jumpstart</u> – This is for anyone who is in a support group, wanting to start a support group, or trying to build up their own support team. I share the principles I've learned in my groups and as a group leader. I teach you how to set up your support group, what key values every support group must have, how to deal with the ups and downs of support, and how to stay strong in your support for the long haul.

<u>21-Day Spiritual Purity Jumpstart</u> – So many of us sexual strugglers have trouble connecting with God. I spend three weeks with you guiding you through purity scriptures and helping you learn how to have a fresh, meaningful relationship with God. This is truly a spiritual jumpstart with a purity focus.

WILL WE EVER MEET?

I hope I get a chance to meet you in the future. Perhaps we will have a chance to work together on your purity. Maybe you will mature and start helping others and we can be ministry brothers or sisters. Maybe I will have a chance to meet you at your church or a men's event. That would be wonderful for me.

If you get a chance, I'd like to hear from you by email. At least we could meet that way. I'd love to hear what this material meant to you and how you're using it. I'd love your feedback. This material comes from my heart and experience at this time. I'm sure I will make modifications in the future. I'd love to hear your thoughts on how I could make it better.

My prayer for you: *Dear God, help this time be a true jumpstart for this special person. Open their eyes to Your truth. Burn into their heart deep motivations and a big vision for purity. Give them the courage to take action steps, come forward, repent, make amends, and follow You in an impure world. Amen.*

Maybe you could pray for me and our ministry too!

My deepest gratitude.

Jeff Fisher

Jeff Fisher
Raleigh, North Carolina
USA

SALVATION

After reading this material, you may have questions about your own spiritual life. Great, your desire to find out more means that God is at work in your life! Knowing God is not about religious rituals. It's about a relationship. You can intimately know God. Throughout this material, I've talked about the vertical connection with God and the horizontal connections with others.

Here are some basics on how to make sure you have the vertical connection right. This presentation of salvation is often called The Roman Road (many of the verses are from the book of Romans). Google "The Roman Road" and you will find an expanded version of it.

God loves you.

> *For God so loved the world that He gave His only begotten Son, that whoever believes in Him should not perish but have everlasting life. John 3:16*

God has a wonderful plan for your life.

> *I have come that they may have life, and that they may have it more abundantly. John 10:10*

Because of your sin, you are separated from God.

> *For all have sinned and fall short of the glory of God. Romans 3:23*

The penalty for your sin is death.

> *For the wages of sin is death, but the gift of God is eternal life in Jesus Christ our Lord. Romans 6:23*

The penalty for your sin was paid by Jesus Christ.

But God demonstrates His own love toward us, in that while we were yet sinners, Christ died for us. Romans 5:8

If you repent of your sin, then confess and trust Jesus Christ as our Lord and Savior, you will be saved from your sins.

For whoever calls on the name of the Lord shall be saved. Romans 10:13

...if you confess with your mouth the Lord Jesus and believe in your heart that God has raised Him from the dead, you will be saved. For with the heart one believes unto righteousness, and with the mouth confession is made unto salvation. Romans 10:9-10

"Repent" – to make a U-turn with your behaviors and attitudes

"Confess" – to acknowledge, to agree with

"Trust" – to put your faith in, to believe with your will

Around the age of 11, I understood in my heart that I needed Jesus. In a simple way, I asked Him to forgive my sins and to come into my life. I grew up in a religious family, but it was not the religion of my family that gave me a relationship with God. It was my simple act of belief and commitment.

Here's a good model prayer you can pray to invite Jesus to come into your life and save you:

Jesus. Thank you for dying on the cross for my sins. I want to follow You. Come into my life and take over. Take control. Help me turn from my sins and choose you. Amen.

A prayer is not magical. You have to mean it in your heart. You have to know you are a sinner and be willing to make a U-turn straight back to Jesus.

** I explain more on the video presentation called "Salvation". Take a look at that when you get a chance.

Hey, if your relationship with Jesus is starting to click, shoot me an email: jeff@puritycoaching.com. I'd love to hear about it.

COUPONS

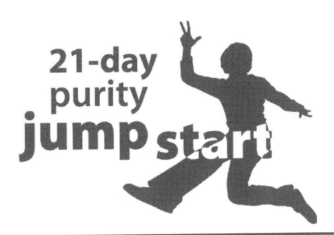

20% OFF – PURITY COACHING

A huge discount on any 4-week coaching package. Includes 1 hour assessment with Jeff and four 1-hour personal purity coaching appointments. Use Code: **COACH20** at checkout at www.puritycoaching.com.

Expires: December 31, 2016

15% OFF - ACCOUNTABILITY

Get help with your accountability - one-on-one help from puritycoaching.com.

Coupon good for any 4, 8, or 12 week package. Use Code: **ACCOUNT15** at checkout at www.puritycoaching.com.

Expires: December 31, 2016

10% OFF – SUPPORT GROUP

Try out one of our online / phone support groups at a discount. You can purchase up to 12 months of support with this coupon. Use Code: **SUPPORT10** at checkout at www.puritycoaching.com.

Expires: December 31, 2016

FREE MONTH – COVENANT EYES
ACCOUNTABILITY / FILTERING SOFTWARE

Covenant Eyes is in our opinion the best internet accountability and filtering software out there. Filters are adjustable. The software works in the background and records your internet usage. Have an accountability report emailed to whomever you choose. Accountability reports and sensitivity levels can be tailored as well.

Use Code: **PURITY** at www.covenanteyes.com to get your first month for free and support our ministry.

NO Expiration Date

AN INTERVIEW WITH THE AUTHOR

Jeff Fisher of PurityCoaching.com

Where are you from?

I'm originally from Austin, Texas. Go Longhorns!

When did you become a Christian?

I accepted Christ as my Savior at 11 years old and started my journey of learning to follow Him.

How did you get into the ministry?

When I was 19 I went on a short-term mission trip to Brazil. I had an opportunity to share my story and talk about the things I was learning from God's Word. I was good at it. Others noticed and suggested perhaps God was calling me to ministry. They were right. After graduating from Texas State University I enrolled at Southwestern Baptist Theological Seminary in Fort Worth. It was fantastic!

Your sexual struggles started after you became a Christian?

Yes. Christians are not immune to sexual struggles and sexual sin. My introduction to porn started when I was 11 or 12. I found a magazine at a construction site, took it home and hid it. My sexual desires were further fueled by the cable TV and movies I watched.

How did your struggles get worse?

I was embarrassed to tell someone. I wanted to stop. I wanted to honor God, but the content I was watching had too great a pull on me. It was exciting. I didn't want to stop, even though I did want to stop. I rarely spoke of my struggles except in moments where I felt terrible guilt. I had moments of getting better, but mostly, I hid and my secret grew.

When did your sexual struggles become uncontrollable?

Strange, I always thought I was in control. It didn't matter that I brought my porn problem into my marriage and into my Seminary life and later into my pastorate jobs. I thought I was always one strong commitment away from tackling my problem. I was deceived and my heart was hardened.

You were a pastor with porn problems?

Yes. Many pastors struggle with pornography. We just don't talk about it until it's too late. I would use my laptop and even my work computer to search for content at moments when I was alone, stressed, or feeling lonely. I needed to be honest and share my struggles with someone. I wish I would have done that much earlier. The consequences to my life would not have been so severe.

What were the consequences?

In 2007, I was working at a denominational office. My mentor pastors discovered porn on my computer and confronted me about it. It was a horrific moment for me. My secret was wide open an exposed. I had nowhere to run. I made a choice to face the truth even though it was very difficult. I had to step down from my newly established church plant, leave the area and seek healing and restoration for my marriage. We moved to the Raleigh, North Carolina area in 2008.

How did the restoration go?

My wife and I are still healing and being restored. Progress was slow at first. The revelation of my sins was actually a relief to me, because my secret was finally out in the open. For my wife, it was a huge blow. There was a lot of anger and pain expressed. There were many difficult conversations. It took many hours in the counseling office to come back to a new level of intimacy.

I was a different, hidden person for the first 10 years of our marriage. My wife knew about some of it and would occasionally ask about my struggles, but I did not share everything. Eventually, before my intervention, I found myself regularly lying to my wife. Lying breaks trust. That's why I have a chapter in this book about practicing truthfulness. It's so critical to finding God's healing.

How did your ministry start?

My wife and I started a website called PorntoPurity.com in 2008. It's still around. It was a place where we could post the resources we were finding and blog about the things we were learning. We felt if we were open about it, we could help others while we healed.

The more we started working with individuals and couples, the more we felt a need to startup our non-profit organization called *Inside Out Ministries*. At the same time, we created PurityCoaching.com. It has been neat to see it grow.

What's your family like?

I've been married now for 18 years. We have two sons, ages 15 and 10, and a beagle named Weezy. My wife is from North Carolina. We met at Seminary and have had many adventures together so far.

Do you attend a group for yourself and do accountability?

Absolutely! I lead my Saturday morning group, but I am very much a participant. I need the support of my brothers on this purity journey. I meet with two accountability partners every Friday for breakfast. They are truly Drill-Down support for me in the best way.

How did the 21-Day Purity Jumpstart come about?

I have been blogging and podcasting about purity since 2008. I also have notebook after notebook at home with thoughts, ideas, and insights from my purity journey. The purity coaching and accountability I have done with my guys has helped me focus my teaching onto several basic topics. Much of the teaching from the 21 days grew organically out of my time with my guys. I have wanted for many years to put these into a book format. I'm finally here.

What's next?

The 21-Day Purity Jumpstart is the first of at least four resources. Coming soon are the 21-Day Accountability Jumpstart, the 21-Day Support Group Jumpstart, and the 21-Day Spiritual Purity Jumpstart. I want to help people get a head start on accountability, obtain support, and become reconnected with God.

Made in the USA
Charleston, SC
06 July 2016